The
World as It
Should Be

Other books by Greg Pierce

The Mass Is Never Ended:
Rediscovering Our Mission to Transform the World, 2007

How Bill James Changed Our View of Baseball, 2007

Diamond Presence:
Twelve Stories of Finding God at the Old Ball Park, 2004

Finding God at Work:
Practicing Spirituality in Your Workplace, 2004

Hidden Presence:
Twelve Blessings That Transformed Sorrow or Loss, 2003

Christmas Presence:
Twelve Gifts That Were More Than They Seemed, 2002

Spirituality at Work:
10 Ways to Balance Your Life On-the-Job, 2001

Of Human Hands:
A Reader in the Spirituality of Work, 1991

For Those Who Work:
Stations of the Cross and Ordinary Mysteries of the Rosary,
1991

Confident and Competent:
A Challenge for the Lay Church, 1987

Activism That Makes Sense:
Congregations and Community Organization, 1984

The World as It Should Be

Living Authentically in the Here-and-Now Kingdom of God

GREGORY F. A. PIERCE

LOYOLA PRESS.
A JESUIT MINISTRY
Chicago

LOYOLA PRESS.
A JESUIT MINISTRY

3441 N. Ashland Avenue
Chicago, Illinois 60657
(800) 621-1008
www.loyolapress.com

Cover design: Larry Cope
Cover image: © Aaron McCoy/Getty Images
Author photo: Jean Clough
Interior globe image: bubaone/iStockphoto.com
Interior design: Mia McGloin

Library of Congress Cataloging-in-Publication Data
Pierce, Gregory F.
  The world as it should be : living authentically in the here-and-now Kingdom of God / Gregory F. Augustine Pierce.
      p. cm.
  ISBN-13: 978-0-8294-2909-1
  ISBN-10: 0-8294-2909-3
  1. Kingdom of God. 2. Christian life—Catholic authors. I. Title.
  BT94.P48 2010
  231.7'2—dc22

                                                                2009035529

Printed in the United States of America
10 11 12 13 14 15 Versa 10 9 8 7 6 5 4 3 2 1

Dedicated to my wife, Kathy,
the love of my life and my partner in building the kingdom.

From the four corners of the earth
    people are coming to their senses,
    are running back to God.
Long-lost families
    are falling on their faces before God.
God has taken charge;
    from now on God has the last word.
All the power-mongers are before God
    —worshiping!

All the poor and powerless, too
    —worshiping!
Along with those who never got it together
    —worshiping!

Our children and their children
    will get in on this
As the word is passed along
    from parent to child.
Babies not yet conceived
    will hear the good news—
    that God does what God says.

—the end of Psalm 22
("My God, my God, why have you abandoned me?")
begun by Jesus of Nazareth on the cross as he died,
from *The Message*, by Eugene H. Peterson

CONTENTS

Foreword: Freely Living between What Is and What Is Not Yet

by John Shea

The World as It Should Be: Living Authentically in the Here-and-Now Kingdom of God is one long invitation to Christians (and perhaps some curious others) to rethink what the kingdom of God means and to act accordingly. There are questions at the end of each chapter so readers cannot escape without personal involvement. As I answered the questions and allowed myself to be pulled into Greg Pierce's exploration of the kingdom of God as a symbol of the way human beings should live together, here are two things that happened to me.

I remembered the first time I meet Langdon Gilkey, then a professor in theology at the University of Chicago. I had decided to do my doctoral dissertation on his work on secular consciousness and religious language. A senior faculty member where I taught warned me against it. "First of all, Jack, he's Protestant and you're Catholic. But most of all, he's alive. What if he doesn't like what you write and refutes you? Stick with the dead." It was sound advice. But I forged ahead anyway.

Over a coffee in the basement of Swift Hall, Professor Gilkey asked me why I wanted to do a dissertation on his work. I said I was interested in theology that was pastorally sensitive and important, and I thought his was. He smiled and said, "That's what my critics say."

This was not going well. So I tried to get a little more intellectual. I asked him if he thought there was one feature of secular consciousness that, if you did not heed it, your theology would not get a hearing. (As best as I can remember, I said it in that clumsy way.) He was quick to respond and the gist of what he said had two points:

- If a theology looked past earthly history to heavenly destiny, it would not get a hearing, even though it promised a happy outcome to difficult lives.
- If a theology held there was an eternal plan that predetermined history, it would not get a hearing.

The reason these types of theology would not be heard is because contemporary people sense in the marrow of their bones that their identity is tied up with their freedom to influence the outcomes of history. If this freedom is not affirmed, their ability to live authentically is compromised. Therefore, what invitations they accept and what invitations they decline are of ultimate importance. As contemporary people, we have to own who we are and how we will live.

Greg Pierce's presentation of the kingdom of God plays into this aspect of contemporary consciousness. He keeps on implying that history is open-ended and human freedom has to create it according to the lure of the kingdom of God. He is like the messenger owl in Harry Potter. He just keeps showing up with that mail. Underneath all the particular questions of the chapters, there is one recurrent question: What are *you* going to do? And if you stall for a moment and seem lost, Pierce has a suggestion: "I maintain an Internet discussion group. If you'd like to join, send me an e-mail at SpiritualityWork@aol.com." It's that owl again.

The second thing that came to mind is another feature of contemporary consciousness—"contrast." Many consider contrast experiences to be the religious experience that is most available to people today. I am not sure of that. I am always leery of analyses that claim too much. But I do know my own contrast experiences have such a ring of truth that they are difficult to walk away from. They have the power to catalyze this old body into action.

Contrast experiences begin when we encounter the world as it is and immediately conclude that it is at cross-purposes with the world as it should be. We are suddenly in the middle of an ethnic hatred that has gone on for centuries, or we see children dying from malnutrition, or we watch self-interest undercut community benefit, and so on. We find the words, "That shouldn't be!" in our mouth before we know we have said them. The *immediacy* of this response is important. We do not reason to it, although reasons may be supplied at a later date. It is the whole person resonating against something that is wrong, "out of joint," or downright evil. This mental, affective, and volitional response is the kingdom of God within us that judges the present as inadequate and impels us to work for the kingdom of God outside us.

Contrast experiences have another important aspect. They are fueled by experiences of a positive sort. We are in the presence of ethnic harmony, or we see well-nourished children, or we watch people sacrifice for one another. These experiences do not lead us to the simple-minded observation that some situations are better than others. They impel us toward the contrast situations with more determination and creativity. We know things can be different, and so we will not settle for the way they are. We decide to become makers of a better history.

As I read Greg Pierce's rendition of the kingdom of God, I knew my contrast experiences had found a dialogue partner. I saw my experiences in the light of the Gospel passages and the Gospel passages in the light of my experiences. There was a great deal of similarity. My experiences supplemented the Gospels, and the Gospels expanded my experiences. Have I been in the grip of the kingdom of God all along and not known it? Is the Gospel vision of the kingdom the thing I need to fully appreciate what my human, indeed my God-given, intuitions attest to? However these questions are answered, the conversation is worth having.

So that is my suggestion to Christians (and those of other traditions) who read this provocative book. Greg Pierce has interpreted the central Gospel symbol of the kingdom of God ("the big idea of Jesus") in a way that speaks to the contemporary consciousness of freedom and contrast. Let it speak to you. It will trigger memories and ideas. Let them come. The conversation is well worth having.

Introduction

When Michelle Obama chose "the world as it should be" as the theme of her speech at the 2008 Democratic National Convention, she was using a phrase from community organizing made popular by Ed Chambers, the executive director of the Industrial Areas Foundation, the leading citizen-organizing network in the United States. Obama was tapping into a strong, nonpartisan desire to make this world a better place for all people.

But she was also coming out of a strong Christian tradition of inaugurating the kingdom of God "on earth as it is in heaven," as Jesus taught us to pray. This tradition has always seen Christianity as good news for the world, a religion that emphasizes work for a just society as the primary vocation or responsibility of each Christian.

This book explores the convergence of those two ideas: the world as it should be and the kingdom of God. It presents things you should know about the Christian concept of the kingdom of God but in the context of the secular task of building the best world possible. Each chapter is followed by questions for reflection or discussion among Christians and another set of questions for dialogue with people outside the Christian tradition.

I argue that the kingdom of God is not a particular system or philosophy. It is neither liberal nor conservative. It does not offer answers to difficult issues of public or social policy—that lies in the realm of human endeavor, where we try to figure out the best way to accomplish what God wants us to do. In pursuing the kingdom of God, two people of good faith can disagree strongly on a particular question of politics or economics or business or family values. If they are both operating in good faith, however, they will seek out the best possible solution—usually some sort of compromise, which is not a bad word in the world as it should be. And they will do so in an atmosphere of mutual respect and understanding. The litmus test for Christians, in any case, is whether decisions are made in the spirit of love, for God and for neighbor.

The kingdom of God is not like any kingdom we are used to on earth. "My kingdom is not from this world" (John 18:36), Jesus told Pilate. So the normal rules of "kingdomness" do not apply. But the kingdom of God is clearly meant to come on earth, starting right now, and so by definition it must involve itself in the secular efforts to build the world into something better, something more like the way the God that Jesus revealed to us would have things.

The kingdom of God is meant for everyone, Christian and non-Christian alike, especially those who are disenfranchised by the kingdoms of this world. This is the good news: we followers of Christ are sent forth to "love and serve the Lord." And the Lord wants each of us to be salt to the earth and light to the world in the everyday activities of life. This is not an option for Christians but the universal vocation to which we are called. And as we exercise it, we will discover that others have that same vocation, even though they do not understand it in Christian terms.

This book offers thirty short chapters on various aspects or elements of the kingdom of God. They are simply stated and explore in detail the practical implications for our daily lives. It is not a book of theology or Bible study. It is a book for Christians, but one that we invite others to read as well, so that we might enter into dialogue with them about the world as it should be.

I am a businessman, a writer, a book publisher, an editor, a son, a brother, an uncle, a godfather (four times), a husband, a father (three times), a friend (many times), a citizen, a community organizer and leader, a Catholic layman, a high school religious education teacher, a former kids' baseball coach, and a Cubs fan. I think people like me should write more books like this, because we know how difficult it is to carry our beliefs out in the world as it is. I approach the kingdom of God as a man who is trying to live my life in a way that makes sense. I think I have found this in Jesus of Nazareth, and I have thrown my lot with him and his vision of what God is really like and how the world can and should be, if enough of us work at it with and through him.

So, explore with me what Jesus meant by the kingdom of God and what it means for us to try to help bring it about. I have tried to keep the chapters short so you can read them on the bus, between innings, or in the car while waiting for your child to finish practice or rehearsal. I have suggested a few questions for reflection or discussion at the end of each chapter, which you are welcome to use, or not, as suits your needs. The quotes from Scripture in this book are from the New Revised Standard Version (accepted by most Catholics and Protestants) or, when noted, from *The Message* by Eugene H. Peterson. I use the latter, which is more of a paraphrasing or retelling than a formal translation, as a way to overcome the familiarity many of us have with Bible verses, which can prevent us from seeing what is really there regarding the kingdom of God.

I had a lot of help with this book. For years I have maintained a group online called Faith and Work in Cyberspace. Many of those people made suggestions that helped identify or clarify the points I am trying to make. They also contributed some of the questions at the end of each chapter to help get you started on your own reflections and discussions. If you would like to join them, simply send me an e-mail at SpiritualityWork@aol.com.

No matter what your religious or political background, I invite you into a discussion of the world as it should be, which we Christians call the kingdom of God.

Gregory F. Augustine Pierce
Chicago

The kingdom of God . . .

. . . was Jesus' big idea.

At the beginning of the Acts of the Apostles, Jesus is still around. Many of us forget this. We think that the Gospels are the story of Jesus and that the rest of the New Testament is what happened after he left. But at the beginning of the Acts of the Apostles, Jesus is present, if only for a couple of verses. Luke says it something like this: Jesus, after he had suffered and died but before he ascended to the Father, met with the disciples over forty days, showing them in many ways that he was still alive and speaking to them about one thing and one thing only (see Acts 1:3).

This is a remarkable statement. Here is a man who has just gone through the most amazing sequence of events any human has ever experienced. First, he suffered terribly and unjustly. The Gospels go to great lengths to point out that Jesus was completely innocent; he is called the Lamb of God—which in the Jewish culture meant a sacrifice without blemish. Finally, he was executed by a most brutal form of Roman torture: nailed naked to a cross until he died of blood loss, shock, asphyxiation, and heart failure.

His disciples had all run away from this horrendous scene, but Mary of Magdala, a couple of other women, Jesus' mother, and the "beloved disciple" stayed.

Three days later, Jesus began appearing to his disciples, apparently starting with Mary of Magdala. They experienced him as truly alive, though in some sort of glorified state. He told Mary not to touch him because he had not yet ascended to the Father; he seemed to walk through walls and locked doors, yet he offered to let Thomas touch his wounds; he cooked some fish and ate it; he appeared to a couple of disciples on the road to Emmaus, although they did not recognize him until they broke bread together.

The point is that Jesus appeared to his disciples many times, showing them in many ways that he was still alive. This alone is pretty amazing. (How many resurrected dead people have visited you?) What is even more interesting, however, is what Jesus chose to speak about with his disciples.

This group had come to realize that they had the Son of God with them. Jesus had suffered brutal torture—some of them had seen it. He had died—some of them had been there. Two prominent members of the Jewish council had taken down the body and laid it in an unused tomb. Pontius Pilate had put guards in front of the tomb to prevent anyone from stealing the body. Then, on Sunday morning, some of the women discovered an empty tomb and didn't know what to make of it. Jesus began appearing to various disciples. They were confused and scared but overjoyed.

It turned out that Jesus soon was going to ascend to the Father. Maybe they didn't realize what this meant immediately, but he made it clear that he was going away. Who knows why? He said, "Nevertheless, I tell you the truth: it is to your advantage that I go away, for if I do not go away, the Advocate will not come to you; but if I go, I will send him to you" (John 16:7). He said that he had to go before them "to prepare a place" for them (see John 14:2–3). So, all they knew is that he was planning to leave them again. This must have made them very sad, but it did lend some urgency to the short time they had with him.

According to the centurion at the crucifixion, "Truly this man was God's Son" (Mark 15:39). Jesus had suffered and died terribly at the hands of the religious and political leaders of his time. The people had turned against him; his own disciples had run away; he had even wondered aloud on the cross whether God had forsaken him. Then miraculously he was raised from the dead. His Father had been faithful to him.

In just a matter of days, Jesus would ascend to the Father and be with him at his right hand for all eternity. He had a short time to be with his disciples, who had not proved a stellar group during their ministry with him and especially through his arrest and execution. They were still afraid, and he had to know that they didn't really grasp what this was all about. He had one last chance with them.

So, what would Jesus talk about during the forty days? Would he teach them how to pray some more? Would he explain the mystery of the Holy Trinity or the Incarnation or the Immaculate Conception? Would he reminisce about the good old days back in Nazareth or describe what it was like to be dead for three days and then come back to life?

He spoke to them about what he had spoken about from the beginning. He spoke to them about what he cared about most, the center of his mission, what he understood his Father wanted him to do, the reason he had come into the world. He spoke to them about what he wanted them to remember most, what he wanted them to do, what he was sending them forth to accomplish: "In face-to-face meetings, he talked to them about things concerning the kingdom of God" (Acts 1:3, *The Message*).

The kingdom of God was Jesus' big idea. It was his vision of the world as it should be, the way his Father would have things, the way things were in heaven. Jesus' entire ministry and mission can be found in the phrase "the kingdom of God," yet it is one of the most misunderstood and sometimes misused concepts in the Christian faith. This book addresses those misunderstandings and misuses and explores what Jesus really had in mind.

What he had in mind was a much different way for human beings to relate to one another and to their world. It was not so much a next-world promise as a prescription for how this world should operate. And it was a radical view indeed, one that has both inspired and repelled millions of people over the past two millennia. Yet it remains every bit as potent and relevant today as it did more than two thousand years ago.

Questions for Christians

1. What do you think Jesus meant by "the kingdom of God"?
2. Why do you think it was so important to him?
3. If you were one of the disciples whom Jesus met with after his resurrection, how would you have reacted to what he told you? (Note: You are!)

Questions for Dialogue with Non-Christians

1. Does the concept of the kingdom of God relate in any way to your tradition's view of the world as it should be? If so, how? How does your tradition talk about these things?
2. What are your concerns about bringing religious values and language into the discussion about how the world should be?
3. Please share your view of how the Christian message, at least as far as you understand it, relates (or doesn't relate) to secular political, economic, and business concerns. Describe how your tradition approaches these same topics.

The kingdom of God . . .

. . . is an unfortunate phrase.

One of the many problems today for people trying to understand the kingdom of God is that the phrase "kingdom of God" itself is foreign to modern speech and sensibilities. Kingdoms are things of the past (Charlemagne was a king; so were Arthur and Frederick and a host of others), or at best they are quaint anachronisms like the British royal family. Another problem with the word *kingdom*, of course, is that it implies a male hierarchy. Even the queen of England is head of a kingdom. Let's face it: most of us would not know a king if we saw one, and if we did, we'd probably giggle or take a picture with our cell phone.

Clearly, Jesus never intended to set up a physical or political kingdom in the sense that we use the term. In fact, it can be argued that the church has made terrible blunders every time it has tried to identify itself with the kingdom of God and then attempted to make that kingdom a political entity, whether it be through the Papal States, the Holy Roman Empire, the Crusades, or the Inquisition. Fortunately, even the most politically minded pope today would no longer equate the kingdom of God with the church. Whatever it is, the kingdom of God is bigger than the church and is out there in the world, where God's kingdom will come, at a time and place nobody knows—not even Jesus.

A contemporary version of the literal view of the kingdom of God is that some Christians try to impose their values and beliefs on others democratically. Working from that mind-set in the debates on abortion, stem-cell research, artificial insemination, gay marriage, and other hot-button issues, they seek secular power to force others to believe as they do. Although it is certainly appropriate, necessary even, that Christians participate in the public debate and the resolution of these issues, this will not be done by grasping secular political power in an attempt to establish some kind of Christian state.

Jesus specifically told Pilate that his kingdom was not of this world:

> "But I'm not that kind of king, not the world's kind of king."
>
> Then Pilate said, "So, are you a king or not?"
>
> Jesus answered, "You tell me. Because I am King, I was born and entered the world so that I could witness to the truth. Everyone who cares for truth, who has any feeling for the truth, recognizes my voice."
>
> JOHN 18:36–37, *THE MESSAGE*

So, Jesus did clearly use the image of a kingdom to describe what he was proclaiming. It made sense back then, because a kingdom ruled by a king was one of the few forms of government people knew about. The Jewish people themselves had a king, although by then he was a lackey of Rome. Certainly Jesus didn't mean he'd be a king like Herod or Caesar, but it is also true that he didn't see himself as a king like David or Solomon. He was a different kind of king, because his kingdom was a different kind of kingdom, not of this world but still in this world.

To avoid all these problems, many have taken to referring to this big idea of Jesus' as "the reign of God." That avoids the kingdom problems, but it raises new ones. *Merriam-Webster Collegiate Dictionary*, 11th ed., defines the verb *reign* as "to possess or exercise sovereign power," or "to exercise authority in the manner of a monarch." This might be acceptable in the abstract and for the long term; certainly God is the ultimate power or authority. But God does not choose to rule as a king or queen. In a sense, *reign* is too weak a word for what the kingdom of God is all about.

Jesus captures the essence of the kingdom of God in the Lord's Prayer when he says, "Your kingdom come, your will be done"— that is, they are the same thing—"on earth, as it is in heaven." How are things done in heaven? Well, we really don't know, do we? In fact, those who say they know, do not. Are the streets paved with gold? Is it a constant beatific vision? We don't know. What we do know is what Jesus thought the kingdom of God would be like here on earth. He talked about it all the time. It was his big idea, and we'll spend the rest of this book exploring what he had in mind.

But we will do so while we use the unfortunate phrase "the kingdom of God." We have to use it for a simple reason: Jesus used it. Over and over again, he talked about the kingdom of God. It was the best image he could come up with, given the time and place in which he was operating. Can we wish he had used something different? Sure. Can we come up with another phrase that might be a little more palatable or politically correct? "the democracy of God" or "the state of forgiveness of God"? Maybe. But we'd better not, for if we do, we might find ourselves off on a tangent that we cannot leave easily. Or we'll spend all our time fighting about what the new image might be. Or we might leave behind most people, who are perfectly comfortable with the words "kingdom of God" and wouldn't know what we are talking about if we changed it.

By the way, the best alternative phrase I've ever heard for "the kingdom of God" came from the pastor emeritus at my parish in Chicago, Father Leo Mahon. He said that the kingdom of God was "the way God would have things." Another phrase can be found at the end of the Nicene Creed, where Christians proclaim that they "look for the life of the world to come." That world to come is the kingdom of God, where the blind see, the captives and oppressed go free, and the poor have good news brought to them (see Luke 4:16–22). The kingdom of God is not heaven or life after death. It is the life of this world, which is still to come. The book of Revelation uses the image of a New Jerusalem to discuss the idea of a better world, a world built on the law of love. So, use any or all of these phrases if you'd like, or make up your own. It doesn't matter anyway. What matters is that we understand what Jesus meant when he talked about the kingdom of God and how we might help bring it about on earth as it is in heaven.

So "kingdom of God" it is. It's an unfortunate phrase because of the baggage it carries, but it is an inspiring vision of how the world could be and has already begun to be. It is the vision of Jesus of Nazareth, who promised that he is "the way, and the truth, and the life" (John 14:6) and chose to name his dream "the kingdom of God."

Questions for Christians

1. If you could think of another phrase or image for the kingdom of God, what would it be? Explain your reasons.
2. What do you think is the essence of the kingdom of God that Jesus preached? Explain.
3. What problems do we get into when we begin to think about the kingdom of God as some kind of earthly kingdom?

Questions for Dialogue with Non-Christians

1. How does your tradition talk about making the world a better place? What images are used?
2. Is there a way for Christians and non-Christians to work together to make the world a better place, without first having to agree on theological language or even specific goals? How?
3. Is there a phrase that all faiths could agree on that would encapsulate the joint mission to the world that they all share? Try to think of one or more.

3

The kingdom of God . . .

. . . *is authentic.*

Authentic is in.
   Time magazine lists authenticity as one of the top new marketing trends:

> Promoting products as "authentic" is serious business these days. You will notice the word and its variants being used to sell just about everything—Stoli vodka (whose new ad campaign urges you to "Choose Authenticity"), Kool cigarettes ("Be Authentic"), the now expired presidential campaign of Mike Huckabee (who called himself an "authentic conservative"), the Web site Highbrowfurniture.com ("Authenticity. Period."), the Claddagh Irish Pub chain (which claims to have an "authentic 'public house' environment," whatever that is) and the state of Maryland, where "even the fun is authentic."
>
> FROM "SYNTHETIC AUTHENTICITY,"
> BY JOHN CLOUD, MARCH 13, 2008

The problem with what passes for authenticity these days is that it is either inauthentic or falsely authentic. You can go to identitee.com and order a T-shirt with a lyric to virtually any song.

This tells people "who you are" and "what you believe." It gives you an "identi-tee" (get it?). At authenticrecordsonline.com you can buy records from Iowa garage bands. You can also purchase their best-selling item, which is a T-shirt that reads "Authentic Records." So you can wear the T-shirt even if you don't actually listen to (or even like) the music.

"We have a hunger for something like authenticity," George Orwell said, "but are easily satisfied by an ersatz facsimile."

Jesus said it this way:

> I'm not interested in crowd approval. And do you know why? Because I know you and your crowds. I know that love, especially God's love, is not on your working agenda. I came with the authority of my Father, and you either dismiss me or avoid me. . . . This is what my Father wants: that anyone who sees the Son and trusts who he is and what he does and then aligns with him will enter real life, eternal life.
>
> JOHN 5:41–43, 6:40, *THE MESSAGE*

The dictionary says that authenticity comes from the Greek word for *self*, implying that those of us seeking to live authentically need to know who we really are. The authenticity that Jesus offers is not false or fleeting but is our truest identity as human beings. For Christians, child of God is the first and foremost identity. If we remember that and act accordingly, we are fully alive right now—and forever.

How do children of God act? They act like Jesus, who always did the will of God the Father: "I am the way, and the truth, and the life. No one comes to the Father except through me. If you know me, you will know my Father also" (John 14:6–7).

So, for Christians, to be authentic is to follow Jesus. But what does that mean in the world as it is?

In his excellent essay "Fake Authenticity: An Introduction" (in *Hermaneut* magazine, December 22, 2000), Joshua Glenn says that true authenticity is "ironically and radically suspicious of all received forms and norms" and "strives to lucidly affirm and creatively live the tension of human reality in all its contingency, ambiguity, and absurdity."

Christians can live with that definition. We must be suspicious of both received and prevailing wisdom until we are sure it meets the law of love, and we have to live in the tension between the world as it is and the world as it should be, with all its "contingency, ambiguity, and absurdity." If we are seeking first the kingdom of God, as Jesus asked of us, we are living authentically in the here-and-now kingdom of God.

This definition of authenticity surprises many people, Christians and non-Christians alike, who think that Christians are anything but suspicious of the status quo. Christians, however, are supposed to look at the world as it is and see it for what it is—full of injustice, suffering, violence, and death. But we also are to have a deep and abiding experience of the world as it should be—full of love, mercy, joy, potential, and life. We are perfectly willing to live with one foot in both worlds, as long as we can do so authentically. The way we do that is by following our leader, Jesus of Nazareth, and his vision for the world, which he called the kingdom of God.

What does this mean practically, in our daily lives? Well, for one thing, we don't seek our authenticity in things or people. We don't allow anything or anyone else to be the measure of who we really are.

Oh, we Christians are as capable as anyone of following fads, and if stone-washed jeans or fruit-flavored martinis are in this year, we'll try them. As do others, we have a sense of history and an eye for quality, and if we think something is authentic, we might be as likely as anyone to buy it. But we don't think that these things make *us* authentic.

Likewise, we don't get our authenticity from other people, including—and maybe especially—our family or our religious leaders. We aren't authentic because our parent or our pastor or even the pope or some other religious leader is (or is not) authentic. Our authenticity comes from within ourselves, to the extent that we stay in touch with who we really are and how we really act.

To do this, most of us try to stay rooted in Scripture and faithful to our religious institutions and practices. We are afraid that if we wander too far from these we may lose our way and become inauthentic or falsely authentic.

But it is not piety and fidelity to doctrine that keep us authentic; it is our action on behalf of the kingdom. "When was it that we saw you sick or in prison?" we'll ask in the judgment. "Truly I tell you, just as you did it to one of the least of these who are members of my family, you did it to me" (Matthew 25:39–40), Jesus will say.

Then, and only then, will we know that we lived a life of authenticity.

Questions for Christians

1. Describe a moment in your life when you felt truly authentic. What do you think caused you to feel that way?
2. Do you see Christians as "ironically and radically suspicious of all received forms and norms"? Explain your answer.
3. How do you stay close to Jesus and his message?

Questions for Dialogue with Non-Christians

1. Do you observe Christians "lucidly" affirming and creatively living the tension between the world as it is and the world as it should be? Explain your answer.
2. What does authenticity mean in your tradition? Give some examples.
3. What is your deepest identity as a human being? How do you stay grounded in that identity in the midst of daily life's hustle and bustle?

The kingdom of God . . .

. . . is in and for this world.

Let's get to the most important question. Is the kingdom of God here and now, in this world, or is it in heaven after we die? For many people, the answer is that the kingdom of God is heaven, the place or state of being we go to after we die. In fact, in the Gospel of Matthew, the kingdom of God is even called the kingdom of heaven, although a better translation might be "the kingdom from the heavens."

There is a strain of Christianity that buys into this understanding. First of all, it seems to fit the facts as we know them. Certainly, the kingdom of God has not come, even after more than two thousand years since the one who inaugurated it died, rose from the dead, and ascended to be with his Father. There is too much pain, sorrow, hate, war, and injustice in the world to argue otherwise. And then there is the reality of death. The mortality rate of the human race is 100 percent, and it always will be. None of us get out alive.

So, the argument goes, if Jesus was promising a kingdom for us, a place where he was, in his words, going to "prepare a place" for us (John 14:2), it must be in the next life, not this one. This definition fits our experience of fragile human existence, and it gives us a sense of relief that, no matter how unjust things are in this life, it will all come out fair after we die. In this scenario, the kingdom of God is our reward for running the good race and keeping the faith, as St. Paul put it (see 2 Timothy 4:7). Those who propose that we can somehow bring about the kingdom of God on earth are wrong. They have been misled into some version of the social gospel, which says that Christianity is all about helping people in this life and not about preparing them for the next.

This is a very persuasive argument, and it is certainly the prevailing wisdom among many Christians and even among non-Christians who try to understand what Christians believe. The problem is that this view of the kingdom of God doesn't seem to mesh with what Jesus had in mind.

The Gospels make it clear that Jesus was on a mission to alleviate injustice, pain, and sorrow of any kind. His story is one of ongoing response to people's needs in the here and now, not after they died. And he genuinely had the belief that, whatever this kingdom of God was, it had already been inaugurated in his ministry and in the community of people he had gathered around him. "The kingdom of God has come near" (Mark 1:15), he proclaimed many times. "The kingdom of God is among you" (Luke 17:21).

And he promised that those who bought into the kingdom of God would be blessed or happy not only in the next life but in this one as well. It was an odd list of people to whom he made this promise: the poor in spirit, the meek, those who mourn, those who hunger and search for justice, the pure of heart, the merciful, the peacemakers, those who are persecuted. "For theirs is the kingdom of heaven," he stated (see Matthew 5:1–10).

Are these people Jesus has just described going to be miserable their entire lives, only to be happy once they get to heaven? He speaks in the present tense, doesn't he? Somehow, by buying into the kingdom of God, these people are blessed right now. Not with some vague promise of happiness after death but with immediate happiness, a peace the world is not able to give but that Jesus does give.

Every single example, parable, and teaching Jesus presents about the kingdom of God focuses on *this* world. The kingdom is about proclaiming the Good News to the poor, the oppressed, the widows, the orphans, the prisoners, the powerless, the disenfranchised—proclaiming not that all the injustices they experience will be corrected after they die but that there is a new movement in the world that will make things better for them right now, when they really need it.

Otherwise, the kingdom of God is just a hollow promise, a magician's sleight-of-hand trick, where happiness is just around the corner if only we hang on and endure our pitiful life now. What kind of message from God would that be? What kind of kingdom would Jesus have been inaugurating? It would have been a sham, and the Son of God would not have wasted his time promoting it.

On the contrary, the kingdom of God is the real deal. It is a road map for the way God would have things in this world—as well as in the next. The whole point of Jesus' life was to reveal to humans, finally and forever, what God is really like and what God wants for us. He showed us what the kingdom of God looks like not only by his teaching but also by how he went about his daily life and how he dealt with real-world situations.

When we look at Jesus, what do we see? We see a man who cared about other human beings, who did everything he could to alleviate suffering and make life more abundant for others. It is neither an accident nor a coincidence that the Gospel of John starts the story of Jesus at the wedding feast of Cana. Despite Jesus' protestations to his mother that his "hour ha[d] not yet come," she knew that it had. "Do whatever he tells you," she says to the servants—and to us (see John 2:1–11). What does Jesus tell us? He tells us to fill the jars of life to the brim and take them to the head chef of the feast. And that chef is the one who realizes just how good the party can be for all the guests.

That is what the kingdom of God is all about: how good the party can be for all the guests. It is apparently the divine will for the human race that we "have life, and have it abundantly" (John 10:10), starting right here, right now, because that is the reason Jesus came. The kingdom of God is in and for this world.

Questions for Christians

1. If the kingdom of God has already begun, what does it look like and where is it located? Provide some specific examples.
2. How can the kingdom of God exist alongside suffering and evil?
3. How is the wedding feast at Cana an example of the kingdom of God? Why do you think the Gospel of John chose to begin Jesus' public ministry with this story?

Questions for Dialogue with Non-Christians

1. To what extent is your tradition focused on this world, and how is it focused on the next, if at all?
2. When you look at the story of Jesus, what do you consider the most important elements of his teaching? Which ones do you disagree with, and why?
3. What great religious or social leaders do you try to follow and emulate? Why?

The kingdom of God . . .

. . . has already begun.

One of the oddest things about Jesus' big idea of the kingdom of God was his insistence that it had already begun: "The time is fulfilled, and the kingdom of God has come near" (Mark 1:15). In fact, one way to understand Jesus is to see him as a man who saw his life's work as inaugurating or proclaiming this kingdom in his own person and mission. "Follow me," he said to his initial disciples, "and I will make you fish for people" (Mark 1:17). Why was Jesus fishing for people? Because the kingdom of God was gearing up, and he needed them to spread the Good News: "The harvest is plentiful, but the laborers are few" (Luke 10:2).

Why would God need people to bring about this kingdom anyway? Why wasn't Jesus enough? Why couldn't Jesus just announce the start of the kingdom over a proverbial loud speaker and have that do the trick?

We Christians don't really know the answer to that. On one level, it seems that an almighty God could have done this without any human help whatsoever. If the kingdom of God is a vastly superior way for humans to live, why would it take millennia for the idea to catch on, and why would humans have to be involved in spreading the news about it? It seems obvious at one level that God shouldn't need our help.

But for whatever reason—and who among us knows the mind of God?—the kingdom of God somehow depends on us. Jesus clearly began the kingdom. He is "the way, and the truth, and the life" for Christians (John 14:6). If we want to know how the world would look if it were the way God would have things, we need only to listen to what Jesus said and to observe what he did. In that sense, the kingdom has already begun. It has already been fulfilled in the person of Jesus of Nazareth, the Christ.

But the kingdom of God also seems to depend on us and on our actions. "For, in fact, the kingdom of God is among you (Luke 17:22)," Jesus said. The kingdom is present in the work of each one of us, to the extent that we act, and whenever we are acting, on kingdom values. The kingdom of God is present every time a parent makes a sacrifice for a child, an employer treats an employee with justice, a voter agonizes over which candidate to vote for, someone stops to help a homeless person or stands up to a bully. When these things are done in the spirit of the Christ, then the kingdom has already begun. But it seems to depend on us doing our part.

There is a famous movie about the kingdom of God, although most people think it is a Christmas film. It runs on television every holiday season, and most people have seen it multiple times—*It's a Wonderful Life*, directed by Frank Capra and starring Jimmy Stewart, Donna Reed, and Lionel Barrymore. It's not a particularly religious film, despite the presence of angels. But it shows us the difference one person can make in the world. George Bailey gets to see what the world might have been like if he had never been born, and in the end, all the people he had touched during his life come together to help him in his time of trouble. The scene at the end, when everyone donates money and sings "Auld Lang Syne" and toasts George Bailey as "the richest man in Bedford Falls," is an image of the world as it should be.

Of course, even in Bedford Falls the kingdom of God had not come completely. Left out of the last scene was Mr. Potter, who apparently is still unrepentant and in need of salvation. There is still work to be done, even though the kingdom of God has obviously begun in the Bailey family's front parlor.

In a parable by Jesus about the final judgment, the king separates people into good (sheep) and bad (goats) and then tells the sheep that they can enter the kingdom because they performed works of mercy:

> Then those "sheep" are going to say, "Master, what are you talking about? When did we ever see you hungry and feed you, thirsty and give you a drink? And when did we ever see you sick or in prison and come to you?" Then the King will say, "I'm telling the solemn truth: Whenever you did one of these things to someone overlooked or ignored, that was me—you did it to me."
>
> MATTHEW 25:37–40, *THE MESSAGE*

The "goats" will complain that if they had known it was the king, they would have done these things all the time. The king will answer them, "I'm telling the solemn truth: Whenever you failed to do one of these things to someone who was being overlooked or ignored, that was me—you failed to do it to me" (Matthew 25:45, *The Message*).

The sheep are those of us who are living the kingdom of God, right now, in our daily lives; the goats are those who are waiting for the kingdom of God sometime in the future. God needs us, although not in the way we need God. *Need* is a concept that really doesn't apply to the divine power of the universe. But God has clearly chosen to use human beings to build this kingdom of God, one brick at a time. That is why Jesus was so persistent about his big idea. He knew he needed his disciples—all of us—to understand that it is our job to help bring about the kingdom. Yes, it's already begun, but it isn't a complete reality yet, and it apparently won't become so, at least not as quickly, if we don't get to work on it.

The point is that we don't have to wait for anyone or anything before we get started. The kingdom has already begun. We know what it is supposed to look like, because Jesus has already showed us. We just need to develop a sense of urgency, to get cracking on building the world as it should be on our jobs, with our families and friends, and in our community and civic affairs. That is where the kingdom will come, if we do our part.

Questions for Christians

1. Give one example of a time you have seen the kingdom of God in action, either in real life or in a book, play, or movie.
2. Does the idea of your being responsible for helping to bring about the kingdom of God scare you or inspire you? Explain.
3. Describe an area of your life in which you need to work harder to make the world more like the way God would have things. What can you do this week to begin doing so?

Questions for Dialogue with Non-Christians

1. What does your tradition say about the perfectibility or improvement of the world?
2. What do you think is the role of human beings in bringing about a better world?
3. How do you feel about working with Christians and others to create the world as it should be? Why do you feel that way?

6

The kingdom of God . . .

. . . *is about action.*

The Christian kingdom-of-God concept can be appealing to those outside the Christian faith because Jesus was very clear about actions speaking louder than words.

Take, for example, his parable of the two sons in Matthew 21:28–32 (different from the two sons and the prodigal father in Luke 15:11–32 but equally illuminating). In Matthew, a father asks the first son to go out and work in his fields. The son says no, then thinks better of it and does what the father asked.

The father asks the second son to do the same. The son agrees wholeheartedly to go but does not do the work. "Which of the two," Jesus asks the chief priests and elders, "did the will of his father?"

"The first," they answer correctly. Not even the chief priests and elders want to admit they are on the side of hypocrisy, although it is interesting that they don't deliver a sermon on the first kid disobeying the fourth commandment with his less-than-respectful attitude.

But then Jesus turns the entire parable on his audience, for he sees something much bigger here than just a couple of mixed-up teenage boys. He says to the religious leaders of his time, "Truly I tell you, the tax-collectors and the prostitutes are going into the kingdom of God ahead of you." Jesus is saying this to the religious leaders of his day, the high priest and the elders. Today it would be aimed at those of us who are in any way self-righteous, no matter our position or reputation in church or society.

What could Jesus possibly mean by such a statement? And how does this observation about prostitutes and tax collectors relate to one kid who says no and then does what his father asks and another kid who says yes but doesn't do what his father wants him to do?

The issue for Jesus appears to be that the chief priests and elders were not listening, first to John the Baptist and then to him. Even when they saw the fruits of the kingdom of God—prostitutes and tax collectors changing their ways—the self-righteous people of his day would not change their minds and believe. Instead, they clung to their religious worldview, even in the face of new evidence and a new vision for the world. For them, this kingdom of God was the subject of intellectual debate. For Jesus, it was a matter of either going into the fields to work or not going into the fields to work. The kingdom of God was about action in the world, not doctrinal beliefs or religious practices.

What would that be like today? Well, in the eyes of many Christian church leaders, the worst people today might be pro-choice politicians. What if people like that suddenly began entering the kingdom of God? What if, for example, politicians who were pro-choice on abortion started to work seriously to lower the number of abortions and to provide adoptive homes for unwanted children? What if they started working on a whole series of "pro-life" issues, including some that pro-life Christians didn't agree with, such as the death penalty or conscientious objection to war? In other words, what if the "bad" people went out into the field and started doing the will of the Father while the "good" people stayed home to debate some more?

Jesus had this in mind when he referred to the prostitutes and the tax collectors of his day. He saw them buying into his vision of a different world, a world as it should be that was based on what he understood to be the will of God, and starting to act in different ways. And he saw the religious leaders of his time refusing to even recognize that these people were changing their actions and to join them in helping to build a better world.

This was clearly not a fight over what happens after death. The prostitutes and tax collectors were not dead or dying, yet they were already entering the kingdom of God. They were entering into a vision of a world that would be organized on different principles, a world in which there would be no need for prostitution or cheating on taxes (or abortions or death penalties or war)—a world based on the law of love. Who wouldn't rejoice that such a world was beginning and join in building it?

Apparently, the religious leaders of Jesus' time would not. He went on to tell another parable in which a capitalist landowner sent his own son to collect some rent owed to him. The landowner says, "They will respect my son." But the tenants killed the son. Jesus asked the religious leaders what they thought the landowner would do to the tenants. "He will put those wretches to a miserable death," they said. Then Jesus turned the story around on them: "The kingdom of God will be taken away from you and given to a people that produces the fruits of the kingdom" (see Matthew 21:33–43).

There it is again. Jesus was interested in action in this world, what he called the fruits of the kingdom, not in good intentions or intellectual belief or adherence to religious rules. If the first son went out to the field and did his work, that was good enough for Jesus. What he couldn't tolerate were those who wanted to talk about it but never went into the field to work: "When the religious leaders heard this story, they knew it was aimed at them. They wanted to arrest Jesus and put him in jail, but, intimidated by public opinion, they held back. Most people held him to be a prophet of God" (Matthew 21:45–46, *The Message*).

This is why the kingdom of God is good news for Christian and non-Christian alike. The kingdom of God is about going out into the fields and doing the work of making the world the way it should be, the way God would have things. It pays very little respect or attention to those who just want to debate whether they should pitch in to help.

Questions for Christians

1. Who would you categorize as the tax collectors and prostitutes of today? Why? What would it mean that they were entering the kingdom of God?
2. Why was Jesus so tough on the chief priests and elders? Where do we see their attitude today? Be specific.
3. When have you acted like the first son? When have you acted like the second son? Explain why in both cases.

Questions for Dialogue with Non-Christians

1. How does your tradition deal with the issue of hypocrisy, of talk instead of action?
2. Are leaders of your tradition resistant to change and working with others outside their own group? Why or why not?
3. What would it mean for people of divergent values to work together to build a better world? How might it happen?

7

The kingdom of God . . .

. . . is about the future.

Why is it important that we understand that Jesus was a Jew? Why couldn't he have been Greek or Roman or Persian? How did being Jewish shape Jesus' big idea of the kingdom of God, even if it was not a prominent theme in the Hebrew tradition?

The answer lies in the straight-line nature of Judaism. What differentiated the ancient Hebrews from their neighbors was that they saw life not as cyclical or as an eternally repeating circle but as a straight line going forward into the future. This was the ultimate "gift of the Jews" to the world, which Thomas Cahill explored in his book of the same title. The Jews had a different way of looking at history and at their place in history, and that way was revolutionary in its implications.

For sedentary people whose life was based on farming, life was a never-ending cycle of planting and harvesting. You finished one cycle and the next one began. You clung to the land and never left it. Your gods were the gods of fertility and rain and harvests, and they were fickle gods indeed.

The Hebrews viewed things differently. From the very beginning, they were a nomadic people, always moving around, always looking for the Promised Land, sometimes getting there, losing it, and finally being put back on the correct path. As a desert tribe, they moved from one oasis or well to the next.

So, theirs was not a cyclical view of the world but a view of life as a pilgrimage that started here and ended there. Abram and Sarai left Ur at the urging of their God and headed out, not sure where they were going but trusting in their new Lord. Moses led the Hebrews out of Egypt, only to take forty years to reach the Promised Land. The Hebrews finally got there, but eventually were taken off into captivity in Babylon. However, the future was always before them and they somehow returned—just as their descendents returned to the land of their ancestors after the Holocaust.

The God of the Hebrews was faithful, not fickle. Their God kept promises and covenants, even when the people did not. God went before them to show them the way. And God would eventually send a messiah who would lead them into the future and to ultimate victory. Jerusalem was the "city built on a hill" (Matthew 5:14) that would become a "light to the nations, that my salvation may reach to the end of the earth" (Isaiah 49:6).

This was the worldview of Jesus. How could it be anything else? He was a Jew. He could see life only as a line of purposeful events going into the future. And so his big idea of the kingdom of God of course would be a path of hope and optimism, not a circle of endless repetition. His God was the God of love, not retribution or fear, a God more like a perfect parent than anything else.

Jesus' Father is, for Christians, the ultimate revelation of the nature of God. That revelation might not have been exactly what the Jewish leaders of his time were looking for. Perhaps they had allowed a little of the cyclical nature of the gods of their neighbors to slip into their thinking and religious practices. Or perhaps they were settling down in their new temple, making accommodations to the Romans, becoming more of a sedentary people. But the Jewish people themselves certainly saw in Jesus' message the core of their own nomadic theology. "Destroy this temple," Jesus said, "and in three days I will raise it up" (John 2:19). How is this possible? Because the temple is not the bricks and mortar but Jesus himself and his mission in and to the world.

If we are ever going to understand the book of Revelation, it is with this linear view of the kingdom of God. The author of Revelation was saying the kingdom of God would ultimately conquer the cyclical kingdoms of the world, including the one that was current then, the Roman Empire. When would that victory occur? Why, in the future of course—when the kingdom would finally be realized.

What are the implications of this view of the kingdom of God for us today? The first thing to recognize is that Christians, at least, cannot be pessimists. History is not doomed to repeat itself. Our problems are not so great that we cannot overcome them. Evil will not win in the end. Why? Because God has promised that it will not, and God is faithful, not fickle. God always goes before us, showing us the way.

Second, the kingdom of God has already begun. It is already within us. Jesus has recruited an army of Christians and fellow travelers in other religions (including our linear-minded Abrahamic allies, the Jews and the Muslims) to dedicate our lives to working to bring about that vision for the world. It may not happen in our lifetime. We understand and accept that. But it is out there, in the future, on a definite path that leads away from where we are now. We see glimpses of it every day.

Questions for Christians

1. Do you see history as more of a repeating cycle or a straight line? Explain. Does your belief in the kingdom of God affect your answer? How?
2. Are you an optimist or a pessimist? Why? Does your belief in the kingdom of God make you more optimistic? How?
3. What are you doing right now in your own life to make the world a better place, a place more like the way God would have things? What else might you do if you thought it would make a difference?

Questions for Dialogue with Non-Christians

1. Do you observe a basic worldview that the three Abrahamic religions share? If so, how would you describe it? If not, how do the different worldviews differ?
2. Where do your own beliefs fall? Are your religious or political views more cyclical or straight line? Why?
3. Are there issues or areas on which you could work together with Christians without compromising your religious beliefs? What are some of those?

8

The kingdom of God . . .

. . . *is about fruitfulness.*

Isn't it strange that the Christian tradition has rather uniformly believed that Jesus was single and had no children (*The Da Vinci Code* notwithstanding)? Most Jewish men at the time would have been married by the age of thirty, and the idea of children as a person's legacy was certainly strong in Jesus' culture.

Most people think that Jesus was celibate because he was some kind of ascetic who forsook sex either as a spiritual discipline or a pragmatic decision based on his understanding of the risks he was taking and the probable end he would endure. However, Jesus was not an ascetic in any other way. He ate and drank with sinners, Pharisees, his disciples—just about anyone he could find. His parables were filled with banquets and feasts, and his first recorded miracle was turning water into wine so that a couple could finish their wedding celebration in style.

The idea of God becoming human to somehow put down or denigrate marriage and family life is pretty ludicrous. Marriage and children are obviously an integral part of the kingdom of God. Jesus said so in many ways, and so has his church.

So, why didn't Jesus have a wife and kids? Maybe he did follow an ascetic spirituality, maybe he realized that his mission would be too hard on a family, or maybe he just never met the right woman. Or maybe, like most of the things the Christ did, he was trying to make an important point through his own example. What could he have been trying to teach us about the kingdom of God?

Perhaps he wanted to demonstrate that fertility is a false god, that having children is not the purpose of life or love. The ancient religions that surrounded the Hebrews were cyclical in nature, based on the idea that life was a regular pattern of planting seeds, cultivating crops, harvesting them, storing the food, rationing it until the next harvest, and making sure to save enough seed for the next planting. This cycle occurred each year and was pretty much the same. Fertility was everything: in the land and in the family. Your success was measured by how fertile your fields were and by how many children you produced—because it took more than a husband and wife to tend the crops and animals. Children were critical resources to survival.

Jesus, however, had no children. He did not express a lot of interest in fertility—neither his own nor that of his disciples. What he was interested in was *fruitfulness*, and that was his basis for judging those who bought into his vision. Thus he told the story of the barren tree:

> A man had an apple tree planted in his front yard. He came to it expecting to find apples, but there weren't any. He said to his gardener, "What's going on here? For three years now I've come to this tree expecting apples and not one apple have I found. Chop it down! Why waste good ground with it any longer?"

The gardener said, "Let's give it another year. I'll dig around it and fertilize, and maybe it will produce next year; if it doesn't, then chop it down."

LUKE 13:6–9, *THE MESSAGE*

The parable of the talents (a unit of money) is another example of the kingdom of God's insistence on bearing fruit. The first two servants double the master's money, and the third digs a hole and hides it out of fear of the master. He is the one who is thrown out amid the "weeping and gnashing of teeth," while the top producer is given that man's share (see Matthew 25:14–30).

What are we to make of these kinds of stories? Jesus seems blissfully oblivious to the question of having children to carry out your legacy. Whereas the promise to Abraham and Sarah was that they would have offspring as numerous as the stars in the sky, Jesus would have no children to carry on his name, his genes, or his kingdom. Instead he would rely on the fruitfulness—not the fertility—of his disciples to bring about the kingdom of God.

Why is this distinction important? It's not that Jesus would have made an argument against having children. He loved children and stated plainly that to enter the kingdom of God a person had to become like a child. In fact, children are the fruit of their parents' love. "Blessed is the fruit of your womb," Catholics pray in the Hail Mary prayer.

In the physical sense, children are not fertile until much later in their lives. However, they bear fruit right away. Who among us has not observed a child blossoming before our very eyes? We expect young people to be fruitful in their studies, as athletes, and in helping other people. At the same time, we desperately hope that they will not be "fertile" until much later in their lives and, we hope, after they are happily married.

The cyclical, fertility-based religions of the ancient world were based on fear. Their gods could grant fertility, but they could also take it away. The God of Jesus, however, wanted everyone and everything to bear fruit. There were no impediments, no pleading for divine favors in Jesus' mind, for his God was the God of love, and love always produces fruit, whether in the form of children or some other manifestation. Everyone is invited to be part of the kingdom of God. All they have to do is be fruitful.

The implications of this are tremendous. It is good news for those married couples who are not able to have children. They are not second-class citizens of the kingdom of God. It also makes single people equal to married people in their spirituality. And it gives new meaning to those who choose a celibate life, not as some kind of ascetic practice but as a celebration of fruitfulness.

Questions for Christians

1. In your mind, what is the difference between fertility and fruitfulness? Does it make sense that the kingdom of God would be more about the latter than the former? Why or why not?
2. Why do you think Jesus never married and had children? What message or example was he trying to give us by not doing so?
3. Do you think that single people or couples without children are second-class citizens in the kingdom of God? Explain your answer.

Questions for Dialogue with Non-Christians

1. How are marriage, being single, and celibacy viewed in your religious tradition?
2. Is there a difference in how your tradition views fertility and fruitfulness? If so, what are some examples?
3. What are the criteria for successful adherence to your religious beliefs? Why?

The kingdom of God . . .

. . . is a peaceable kingdom.

Christians should not have an ounce of self-righteousness left in us. We have done so much harm in the world, often in the name of our religion itself, that we can only beg our fellow human beings (and our God) for forgiveness.

None of this is Jesus' fault, of course. He showed us the way by his teaching and his own example, and he envisioned a kingdom of God on earth based on the law of love. He would never have participated in things like the religious wars and persecutions among Christians or between Christians and non-Christians. He would have been sickened by crusades and inquisitions and forced conversions.

Nor would he have been in favor of secular wars and violence. It's hard to imagine him as a general or even a private in an army of any type. In fact, he probably wouldn't have been attracted to police work either. He was a nonviolent type of person, a man of peace. It's hard to read the Christian Scriptures and come to any other conclusion. For Jesus, the kingdom of God was a peaceable kingdom. He went to his death rather than fight his enemies. He told us we had to love our enemies, even if—and especially because—they hate us.

So, why are not all followers of Jesus pacifists? We probably should be, but our faith is too weak. We imagine that Jesus couldn't have meant us to take him literally on this issue. Or even if he did, we have decided that it is impractical and maybe immoral for us not to fight back when we are threatened or attacked. So we come up with theories of just war and other explanations for the need for an acceptable level of police and military power. Who among us doesn't want the Secret Service to protect the life of our president, for example, or the Department of Homeland Security to prevent another attack like that of September 11? And when we see that genocide has taken place or is taking place—in Germany, in Cambodia, in Rwanda, in Darfur—we are glad we have a military force that can stop it and are upset when they don't. We pray for the members of our congregations who are in the military or law enforcement and hope that they will remain safe.

But the bottom line is this: we Christians should never feel too comfortable with our positions on all these issues, because Jesus' view of the kingdom of God was clearly one of love, forgiveness, and peace. "Blessed are the peacemakers" (Matthew 5:9), he said in the Sermon on the Mount. For Christians at least, war and police action should be a last resort, one that we choose after all other possibilities have been exhausted and, even then, with a reluctance bordering on refusal.

In the world as it should be, according to the Christ, there is no need for armies or police forces (except maybe to direct traffic and get cats down from trees). We Christians, however, like all other humans, do not live in the world as it should be. We live in the world as it is. In the world as it is, there are people doing horrendous things who need to be stopped by almost any means necessary. And so we Christians support our military and police and the entire law enforcement infrastructure, as most other people do. We may try to remain vigilant about protecting the innocent and making sure we use our power only for good. We may insist on supporting and following international law in the conduct of wars and the protection of civil rights for citizens and noncitizens alike. We may even argue, as did Pope Paul VI, that "if you want peace, work for justice."

But the one thing we should not do is claim that we are following Jesus' idea of the kingdom of God when we compromise our stand on violence. It appears that Jesus did not have a bone of self-preservation in his body, that he thought violence was not an option for us—starting right now—either as individuals or as a society.

So, where does this leave most of us Christians today? Well, in some ways, we are hypocrites for saying we have faith when we really don't practice the faith Jesus practiced. He apparently believed that you took up your cross and followed it to its logical end rather than returning violence for violence. We Christians, in contrast, sometimes agree with this idea in the abstract, but when it comes down to it, we'd rather stand up to the evil people of the world and beat them at their own game. We are weak. We are sinners. We are ordinary humans.

But we are talking in this book about the world as it should be, the kingdom of God, where things are done on earth as they are in heaven. So, if we're serious about our beliefs at all, as Christians we will always have a pacifist streak in us. We should feel uncomfortable with every use of violence, no matter how noble the cause. We should constantly be vigilant about the use of our military and police power and try to minimize it in every instance. We should work for peace in every imaginable way, whether by trying to get two neighbors or family members to reconcile or by trying to help solve the seemingly intractable problems in the Middle East or in Africa or in our own country.

The true Christian's instinct is to give in, to turn the other cheek, to forgive and forget, to live and let live. In the kingdom of God, the lions lie down with the lambs, and the Christians should be the lambs in that situation.

Questions for Christians

1. Do you think Jesus was a pacifist? Why or why not?
2. When you support the use of violence in your own life or in society, how do you reconcile it with your Christian beliefs? Do you think you are following the teaching and example of Jesus, or do you justify it in another way? Explain your answer.
3. Do you agree that "the true Christian's instinct is to give in, to turn the other cheek, to forgive and forget, to live and let live"? Give examples that support your position.

Questions for Dialogue with Non-Christians

1. How does your tradition talk about peace in the world? Is it absolute or conditional? Explain.
2. What is your view of the history of Christianity regarding issues of war and violence? Do you consider Christians hypocrites on this issue? Why or why not? How would you judge your own tradition on these issues?
3. Can the world ever be truly at peace? What would that look like? How could it be accomplished?

10

The kingdom of God . . .

. . . *is one big thriving family.*

Jesus' vision of the world was not one of every person for him-
or herself. First of all, he was a Jew, and Jewish people have
never thought that way. They were always God's chosen people,
not God's chosen group of isolated individuals. The Exodus
established this relational and communal aspect of Judaism, the
Babylonian captivity restored it, and the Holocaust confirmed it.

Jesus would never have thought individualistically. In fact,
he took relational and communal thinking to its ultimate end
by declaring that all members of the human race were sons and
daughters of God, whom he referred to as Abba ("Father"). When
he taught us to pray, it began "Our Father"—not "My Father."
This God whose kingdom is to come is—in Jesus' mind—more
like a good parent than anything else, and good parents build
relationships with and between their children and build com-
munities called families. So, whatever the kingdom of God was
going to be, it would look a lot like one big thriving family.

Whenever Jesus talked about God, his primary frame of reference
was his own relationship with the Father and the Holy Spirit. This

relationship was infinitely intimate, loving, and trusting. It took the church about three hundred years (at the Council of Nicaea and other meetings) to finally articulate what we Christians believe that relationship to be. We still call it a mystery when we try to describe or explain it to ourselves or to others. In fact, the doctrine of the Trinity is one of the major stumbling blocks for people trying to accept mainline Christianity and for us Christians trying to explain our faith to others—especially to our Jewish and Muslim brothers and sisters. For on the surface, it certainly sounds as if we believe in three equal Gods, which would undermine the monotheism (belief in one God) that is basic to all three Abrahamic religions (Judaism, Christianity, and Islam).

But the early Christians had a problem that only the Trinity could solve. They had this man, Jesus, who talked about the Father and the Holy Spirit with such power, authority, and intimate knowledge that they could only conclude that he himself was God. The opening to the Gospel of John says it this way:

The Word was first,
    the Word present to God,
    God present to the Word.
The Word was God,
    in readiness for God from day one.
Everything was created through him;
    nothing—not one thing!—
    came into being without him.
What came into existence was Life,
    and the Life was Light to live by.
The Life-Light blazed out of the darkness;
    the darkness couldn't put it out.

                    JOHN 1:1–5, *THE MESSAGE*

The Nicene Creed, which is still accepted by virtually all who call themselves Christian, states, "I believe in the Holy Spirit, the Lord, the giver of life. He proceeds from the Father and the Son, and with the Father and the Son he is worshipped and glorified."

What has any of this to do with the way the world should be? Simply this: Jesus could not have proclaimed the coming of a world in which things were not as they are in heaven, and heaven had always been a relational and communal existence. In Christian thought, God is not an individual but is three-in-one, what we have dubbed "the Trinity," at all times, each person of the Trinity relating to the other two in community as absolute equals. The Trinity is Jesus' model for the kingdom of God, and that is what we are called to help build here on earth.

"Impossible," you say? Of course it is. But for Jesus, "for God all things are possible" (Mark 10:27). "Utopian," you cry? It is, literally, nowhere. But, Jesus assures us over and over that the kingdom is coming and, in fact, has already begun. How can he be so sure? Because that is his experience of God: God is, always has been, and always will be relational and communal. Because humans are made, according to Genesis, in the image of God, then we are capable of community as well.

What are the practical effects of this Trinitarian belief on the world as it should be? First of all, the kingdom of God is big on equality. In fact, when the disciples started scheming about who would be first in the kingdom, Jesus turned the argument on its head and promised that "the last will be first, and the first will be last" (Matthew 20:16). Second, the kingdom of God will be most like a family. Family is the place of unconditional love, of self-sacrifice, of forgiveness, and of reconciliation. Finally, the kingdom of God will be the best news for the poor and oppressed, because in a good family it is the "least of these who are members of my family" (Matthew 25:40) who should be cared for the most.

My pastor emeritus, Reverend Leo Mahon, put it this way in his book *Jesus and His Message: An Introduction to the Good News*:

> Allow me to point out a human situation that will help us understand Jesus' idea of the kingdom or reign of God. Let's say you are a loving parent of seven children. You are dying of cancer and have but a few days to live. You gather your adult children around your bed to bid them farewell. Perhaps one is disabled, another is very troubled and has been in and out of jail, and a third is a single parent struggling to raise three children. Your other four children have good marriages and healthy children and are in good financial shape.
>
> What dying wish would you express, then, to your seven children? I believe you might say something like this: "Love one another. Be good to one another, especially to those of you who need more care. Always forgive one another. Never give up on one another. Stay together as a family. If you do all this, you will be living the way I want you to live."
>
> Now, suppose your children responded positively and permanently to your dying request. Over the years, they would become a beautiful family, saving themselves from discord and ruin, and inspiring other families to do the same. But if your children ignored your words and refused your dying request, the results would be tragic. Those children who needed loving care from the others would not get it and would sink into despair and bitterness. Those who were well off would become more and more selfish and self-righteous. All of your grandchildren would grow up in a poisonous atmosphere. The evil would grow fast and last for a long time.

Thus it is with the kingdom of God. If human parents want good things for their loved ones, would that not also be the desire of God, who Jesus taught us was most like a loving parent? It is the will of God that all human beings live now—in this world—in peace as members of the same family, forgiving one another, sharing with one another, taking care of the ones who need it most, regarding all members of the family as valuable and as equals. That is what Jesus meant by the kingdom of God, and that is why he said it had already begun in his person.

Questions for Christians

1. How do you respond to the idea that the doctrine of the Trinity describes God as relational and communal? What practical effects might this belief have on your daily life?
2. What are the implications for you of the kingdom of God being like one big thriving family?
3. Does equality in the kingdom of God mean that everyone has exactly the same things? If not, what does it mean to you?

Questions for Dialogue with Non-Christians

1. Is your tradition's image of God—or humanity—individualistic or relational and communal? What does that mean in how you live your daily life?
2. How are the poor and the oppressed treated in your tradition? Why?
3. What do you think about the idea of all humans being part of one big thriving family?

II

The kingdom of God . . .

. . . *is about repentance, forgiveness, and reconciliation.*

One of the key elements of the Christian view of the world as it should be is that repentance, forgiveness, and reconciliation are plentiful and easily accessible. "If you forgive the sins of any," Jesus told his disciples, "they are forgiven them; if you retain the sins of any, they are retained" (John 20:23). And in the Lord's Prayer Jesus taught us to pray that we will be forgiven our sins and failings to the same degree as we forgive the sins and failings of others.

Christians are not looking for a world in which everyone is perfect. First of all, that is probably impossible, given human nature. People are going to make mistakes—big ones and little ones— even when the kingdom finally becomes reality. Perhaps this is why Jesus said that even he did not know when the kingdom would actually arrive.

Second, a perfect world is probably a boring world. Part of the beauty of the universe is its unpredictability. And some of that unpredictability comes, in part, from the actions of human beings who are constantly pushing the envelope of life—trying new things and making mistakes in the process.

We Christians recognize that grace is undeserved, that God's help, inspiration, and forgiveness are readily available and always free—that is, not contingent on our state of worthiness or our lack thereof. When Christians gather to pray, one of the things we always do is repent. We don't take a show of hands as to who has sinned and who has not. We assume that we have all done wrong things and are sorry for them, and so we ask for forgiveness, knowing that it is always given.

In perhaps his greatest parable, one that some people say contains the entire message of the Gospels, Jesus tells the story of a father's forgiveness of one son and his challenge to his other son to let go of his anger and sense of injustice and come in and join the reconciliation party (see Luke 15:11–32.)

We call this the parable of the prodigal son, but really it is about a prodigal father, who is too liberal with his fortune and his love and his forgiveness. The father, of course, is God, the Father of Jesus. The sons are all of us, men and women alike.

The father in this story is certifiably crazy. In the world as it is, he would have been declared incompetent and his finances would have been put under a court-ordered supervisor. But of course this is a story about the kingdom of God, and in Jesus' vision of the world as it should be, all that is important is love.

Anyway, the younger son asks his dad to give him his inheritance right then, and the dopey guy does it. He must have known that his kid would waste it all. What father in his right mind would let his juvenile-delinquent son have that much money?

Predictably, the young man promptly blows through the dough and finds himself tending pigs in a foreign land. He thinks,

> How many of my father's hired hands have bread enough and to spare, but here I am dying of hunger! I will get up and go to my father, and I will say to him, "Father, I have sinned against heaven and before you; I am no longer worthy to be called your son; treat me like one of your hired hands."
>
> LUKE 15:17–18

The dad takes back the son, but not as a servant. He takes him back as a son, puts a ring and a robe on him, and kills the proverbial fattened calf in celebration of the boy's return. You see, in the kingdom of God, repentance, forgiveness, and reconciliation are the norm. They are expected—the way business is supposed to be done.

The older son, however, does not get this. He has not yet bought into the kingdom way of thinking. He is still living in the world as it is, and in the world as it is there are limited resources and people don't reconcile so easily. Grace is expensive in his world, and there is only so much of it to go around.

The father tries to make the older son understand this: "But we had to celebrate and rejoice, because this brother of yours was dead and has come to life; he was lost and has been found" (Luke 15:32).

The older son is not convinced. He is holding his brother in his sin, and in the process he is holding himself there as well. At the end of the story, we don't know whether the son goes in to join the party.

Many of us have been the younger son—doing something stupid, repenting (even if for the wrong reasons), and being reconciled with God and with our loved ones. The key to this story, however, is that we have all been the older son as well—refusing to forgive others for something they have done, putting our desire for fairness and punishment of wrongdoing before our willingness to be reconciled.

"What kind of world as it should be would it be if we let people like the prodigal father and the prodigal son run things?" you might ask. And you would be right. That is why the kingdom of God begins *between* the world as it should be and the world as it is. But Jesus' view of God and the way God would have things is clear: God always comes down on the side of repentance, forgiveness, and reconciliation. This is what God does. Apparently, the heavenly Father Jesus describes doesn't know any other way.

The practical implications for us Christians as we try to help build the world as it should be are obvious: we are always going to be in favor of giving people another chance; we are always going to admit that we have done bad things ourselves; we are always going to be willing to be reconciled with others—no matter what they, or we, have done. Does this make us naive or impractical or unfair? In a sense, it does. But more important, it leads us to be less judgmental, more understanding, and best able to bring warring or hate-filled enemies together to make a better world.

Questions for Christians

1. What are your honest reactions to the prodigal son parable? With which character do you most identify? Why?
2. Would easily accessible repentance, forgiveness, and reconciliation be any way to run the world? Explain your answer, with examples.
3. How do you think the tensions between the world as it is and the world as it should be can be resolved? What is your role in doing so?

Questions for Dialogue with Non-Christians

1. How are repentance, forgiveness, and reconciliation handled in your tradition? What about the idea of punishment for sins?
2. Do you have a story or parable about forgiveness in your tradition?
3. How can people who have different views on basic questions of fairness and justice work together?

12

The kingdom of God . . .

. . . *is nonjudgmental.*

I t will surprise many Christians and non-Christians alike that the kingdom of God is nonjudgmental, because often it seems that the kingdom of God is all about making judgments. But the kingdom of God is decidedly nonjudgmental. In the Scriptures there are many situations in which God is judging others, and rightly so, and certainly in Christian history there has been judgment galore, which continues to this day. Christians also have a belief in the Last Judgment, when everyone will get his or her comeuppance, and the entire book of Revelation seems to be one big war over who gets to judge whom.

But at a very basic level, the kingdom of God is not about judgment. "Do not judge, so that you may not be judged," Jesus advised (Matthew 7:1). And in the famous passage from the Gospel of John, he laid it out pretty clearly: "God didn't go to all the trouble of sending his Son merely to point an accusing finger, telling the world how bad it was. He came to help, to put the world right again" (John 3:17, *The Message*).

For Jesus, it seems that any judgment made about people is one they bring on themselves by not embracing his vision of the kingdom: "Anyone who trusts in him is acquitted; anyone who refuses to trust him has long since been under the death sentence without knowing it. And why? Because of that person's failure to believe in the one-of-a-kind Son of God when introduced to him" (John 3:18, *The Message*).

In the Gospel of John (and in none of the other Gospels), we find the story of a woman caught in adultery (see John 8:1–11). The religious leaders of the day, who are focused on the rules and the people who break them, bring the woman before Jesus and say that the law of Moses requires that she be stoned to death.

Jesus bends down and writes with his finger in the dirt. The theologian John Shea points out that the only other person to write with a finger in the Scriptures is God, who wrote the Ten Commandments on stone tablets. This is not a coincidence, for the author of the Gospel of John clearly believes that Jesus is the Son of God. Here is how the exchange goes:

> They kept at him, badgering him. He straightened up and said, "The sinless one among you, go first: Throw the stone." Bending down again, he wrote some more in the dirt.
>
> Hearing that, they walked away, one after another, beginning with the oldest. The woman was left alone. Jesus stood up and spoke to her. "Woman, where are they? Does no one condemn you?"
>
> "No one, Master."
>
> "Neither do I," said Jesus. "Go on your way. From now on, don't sin."
>
> JOHN 8:7–11, *THE MESSAGE*

This story creates a conundrum: if the kingdom of God is not about judging others, then how are we ever going to know what it stands for? Is the kingdom of God pro-prostitution or anti-prostitution? Pro-gun or anti-gun? Pro-life or pro-choice? And doesn't the kingdom of God have laws and courts and judges and jails? If not, how is it ever going to operate? How can we have the world as it should be without laws, which imply judgment and punishment?

Again, we find ourselves smack dab between the world as it is and the world as it should be. There is no question that in the world as it is there are bad people who need to be judged, and some of them need to be put in jail. And not to condemn racism or sexism or ageism or prejudice in all its forms is clearly wrong. Who would follow a philosophy that says, "Everything is equal, no one is to blame, we can't hold anyone accountable for not abiding by our laws and morality"? In fact, some of the greatest "saints" of all time, from Paul to Joan of Arc to Martin Luther King Jr. to Mother Teresa confronted evil every chance they got.

Jesus himself did the same. He was merciless on the Pharisees and Sadducees, and he seemed unafraid to tip over the tables of the money changers in the temple. Therefore, we presume he wants us to do the same as well, and so we "fight" for justice and in the process often condemn those who don't agree with us.

But the key to the kingdom of God's nonjudgmental nature is precisely that it is a description of the world as it should be. By the time the world becomes "as it is in heaven" we will have no need for judgment, because people will already have brought judgment on themselves. People in the kingdom of God will not condemn others, because they will recognize that they have all sinned but are now on the same page. Once she enters the kingdom of God, the woman caught in adultery will no longer sin, and therefore she will have no need of condemnation. The same will be true of all of us.

So, when we say that the kingdom of God is not judgmental, Christians are saying that in the world as it should be *no one* will be judgmental. We may still have differences of opinion, as people do about art and music and literature and politics and economics, but there will be no stoning, no self-righteousness, no sense of being holier than thou—nor will there be inequality or injustice or war or poverty.

That's when we'll know that the kingdom of God has come, that the world as it should be has arrived.

Questions for Christians

1. Who needs to be judged in the world as it is, and why? How do you reconcile this need with Jesus' words and example?
2. Whom are some of the people you admire—in church or society, past or present—whose trademark has been a tireless confrontation of evil in this world? Have their actions included judgment or condemnation of others? Explain.
3. What would a world that was nonjudgmental look like?

Questions for Dialogue with Non-Christians

1. In your tradition, how and why do you judge people, if at all?
2. Do you consider Christians particularly judgmental or nonjudgmental? Why?
3. How would it be possible to create a world in which people differed but did not judge one another? How would such a world function? Would that be appealing to you? Why?

The kingdom of God . . .

. . . *is an imperative verb.*

Go. Ask. Feed. Stay awake. Proclaim. Seek. Find. Look. Bring. Take. Hear. Do. Come. Repent. Baptize. Understand. Be prepared. Believe. Work. Change. Come and see. Pray. Love.

The kingdom of God is an imperative verb.

For many years I have taken our family dog, Chewy, for a walk twice a day. Most of those years, I resented this task. I never wanted a dog—my wife and kids did. But none of them would take the dog for a walk on a regular basis, so I did.

Chewy and I always take the same route: up one side of our block and down the other. She has to sniff every tree and fire hydrant along the way, and I wasted a lot of my life pleading with her, "Come on."

One day I was thinking about the kingdom of God. (My children will roll their eyes when they read that last sentence, but it's the truth.) Suddenly I realized that I had an opportunity to help make the world more like it should be, more like the way God would have it, during those daily walks. So I started picking up the trash on the block. There wasn't a lot of it, but there was always some. Teenagers from the neighborhood would congregate behind our neighbor's bushes to have their first illegal beers and would leave behind a few cans or bottles. Smokers would crush their cigarette butts in the street or on the sidewalk. People would leave unsolicited flyers or newspapers in their driveways. Branches would fall from trees during a storm.

Anyway, I just started picking up the debris every morning and evening. I did so as a spiritual discipline, if you will, as a way of reminding myself that the kingdom of God is an ongoing and ever-present job.

There were at least two results from this practice. First, I began to actually enjoy walking the dog. I'm not saying I never complained about it again, but it did become a more meaningful, and therefore more enjoyable, task. Second, my block in Chicago is one of the cleanest in the world! To me, this is aesthetically pleasing. I'm not sure anyone else notices, but I do.

This practice also reminds me that the kingdom of God is an imperative verb. That is, it is something that needs to be done in order to exist. It is not just some article of belief or intellectual comprehension; it must be put into action at all times and in all places. Walking the dog and cleaning the block each day remind me of this, and if I can remain aware of it the rest of the day, I look for other opportunities to make the world a little bit of a better place in the midst of my daily routines.

If you read the Gospels, it is amazing how often Jesus was telling his disciples to do something. In his vision of the kingdom, the worst thing that can happen is for people to be idle. For example, the key to the parable of the workers hired at different times is that the employer (God) hates to see anyone not working (see Matthew 20:1–16).

For Jesus, it was all about the vineyard. He was the vine, and we are the branches. If his vision for the world was going to bear fruit, his followers were going to have to work at it, even on the Sabbath. There is a story of an invalid who sat near the pool of Bethesda for thirty-eight years, waiting to be cured. Jesus asked him a funny question: did he really want to be cured? The man complained that he didn't have anyone to put him into the water when it stirred, but Jesus would have none of his excuses. He told him: "Stand up, take your mat, and walk" (John 5:8), and the man did.

The scandal for many at the time was that Jesus told the man to do something on the Sabbath, even something as fundamental as carrying his bedroll. But for Jesus, doing something is what the kingdom of God is about: "My Father is still working, and I also am working" (John 5:17).

The work that we Christians are ordered to do is the work of God. It involves everything we do, from walking the dog to curing AIDS. Jesus said: "I'm telling you this straight. The Son can't independently do a thing, only what he sees the Father doing. What the Father does, the Son does" (John 5:19, *The Message*). What does the Father do? As Father Don Headley of my parish often says, God does two things: God creates the world and makes it a better place, and God forgives people and frees them from whatever oppresses them. So that is what Jesus does.

And Jesus sends us to do the same. When he finally appeared to the assembled disciples all together after his resurrection, he said to them: "Peace be with you. As the Father has sent me, so I send you" (John 20:21). Then he breathed on them (and us) and said, "Receive the Holy Spirit. If you forgive the sins of any, they are forgiven them; if you retain the sins of any, they are retained" (John 20:23).

So, we've got the Holy Spirit, the spirit of God, within us. We've also got our marching orders: we are to do the work of the Father, which is to bring about the kingdom of God, on earth as it is in heaven. It takes work, even on the Sabbath, and it begins, curiously enough, with forgiving ourselves and others. That is the world as it should be. It is an imperative verb.

Questions for Christians

1. Why does building the kingdom of God begin with forgiveness? What are some examples?
2. What is the difference between believing in the kingdom of God and working to bring it about?
3. Name as many imperative verbs from the Gospels as you can remember or find. What, if anything, do they have in common?

Questions for Dialogue with Non-Christians

1. In your tradition, what is the connection between work and the world as it should be?
2. How does your tradition view the Sabbath or the idea of rest from work? Are you allowed to do good deeds on the Sabbath? Explain.
3. In your tradition, what are the imperatives for people? That is, what are the things they are required to do to remain faithful to your vision for the world?

The kingdom of God . . .

. . . *is full of joy.*

Happy, happy, joy, joy," my wife, Kathy, will say in jest, often when life has gotten difficult in some way. In doing so, she is describing another unlikely element of the kingdom of God: it is full of joy.

Joy would seem unlikely in a world so filled with sorrow, pain, and death. To be human is to suffer, at least part of the time. So, what's with all the euphoria among Christians? Why do we claim to be happy, even when we are sad?

Jesus described this paradox in his foundational Sermon on the Mount, which is found in Matthew's Gospel, the most organized of the four Gospels. This sermon may be a summary of Jesus' teaching, because parts of it are repeated throughout the Gospels.

The sermon starts off very clearly: "Change your life. God's kingdom is here" (Matthew 4:17, *The Message*). Then Jesus launches into his eight beatitudes, which comes from the Latin word *beatus*, which means "happy." Thus, the word *blessed* might best be translated as "happy" or "joyful." Eugene Peterson's rephrasing of the Scriptures offers an opportunity to look at the beatitudes in a fresh way:

> You're blessed [happy] when you're at the end of your rope. With less of you there is more of God and his rule.
>
> You're blessed [happy] when you feel you've lost what is most dear to you. Only then can you be embraced by the One most dear to you.
>
> You're blessed [happy] when you're content with just who you are—no more, no less. That's the moment you find yourselves proud owners of everything that can't be bought.
>
> You're blessed [happy] when you've worked up a good appetite for God. God's food and drink is the best meal you'll ever eat.
>
> You're blessed [happy] when you care. At the moment of being "care-full," you find yourselves cared for.
>
> You're blessed [happy] when you get your inside world—your mind and heart—put right. Then you can see God in the outside world.
>
> You're blessed [happy] when you can show people how to cooperate instead of compete or fight. That's when you discover who you really are, and your place in God's family.
>
> You're blessed [happy] when your commitment to God provokes persecution. The persecution drives you even deeper into God's kingdom.
>
> Not only that—count yourselves blessed [happy] every time people put you down or throw you out or speak lies about you to discredit me. What it means is that the truth is too close for comfort and they are uncomfortable. You can be glad when that happens—give a cheer, even!—for though they don't like it, I do! And all heaven applauds. And know that you are in good company. My prophets and witnesses have always gotten into this kind of trouble.
>
> MATTHEW 5:1–12, *THE MESSAGE*

We Christians are happy because we have a different way of looking at the world and the human condition. Christians do not deny the bad things of life, nor do we expect them to disappear just because we believe that the kingdom of God has begun. No one following a man who was tortured and executed, even though he was clearly innocent, can ever deny the injustice of the world as it is. And even in the world as it should be, Christians do not expect everything to be perfect—at least not until the end or maybe in the next life, as we call life after death.

What Christians believe is that Jesus' dream of the kingdom of God—which has already begun and is still to come on earth—offers humanity hope that things don't have to be the way they are, that by changing how we view and do things we can be "salt of the earth" and a "light of the world" (see Matthew 5:13–14). And this makes us pretty happy. It gives new meaning to our existence and even to our trials and struggles.

This hope is not naive. We see the problems of the world—at times, they seem absolutely overwhelming. But then we realize that we are not alone, that we have a plan for dealing with things, and that God is on our side—not to defeat our enemies or put us in charge but to bring about a new way of doing business that begins with us. If people don't like it (and many won't), they will oppose us and possibly persecute us. Even that will make us happy, because we'll know that we are getting through to them and we'll have hope that we can make a difference in the world.

Václav Havel, the former president of the Czech Republic, captured the true meaning of hope in this famous quote:

> Hope is a state of mind, not of the world. . . . Either we have
> hope or we don't; it is a dimension of the soul, and it's not essen-
> tially dependent on some particular observation of the world or

estimate of the situation. Hope is not prognostication. It is an orientation of the spirit, an orientation of the heart; it transcends the world that is immediately experienced, and is anchored somewhere beyond its horizons. . . . Hope, in this deep and powerful sense, is not the same as joy that things are going well, or willingness to invest in enterprises that are obviously heading for success, but rather an ability to work for something because it is good, not just because it stands a chance to succeed. The more propitious the situation in which we demonstrate hope, the deeper the hope is. Hope is definitely not the same thing as optimism. It is not the conviction that something will turn out well, but the certainty that something makes sense, regardless of how it turns out.

It is this hope that makes Christians blessed. Happy, happy, joy, joy.

Questions for Christians

1. How happy are you now? What about when things aren't going so well? Explain.
2. Which of the beatitudes from the Sermon on the Mount is your favorite, and why?
3. Have you ever been persecuted in any way for being a Christian? If yes, how? If not, why not? (Or answer this old question: If being a Christian were a crime, would there be enough evidence to convict you?)

Questions for Dialogue with Non-Christians

1. In what ways and situations, if any, do you find Christians happy or blessed? Explain.
2. What about your tradition makes you happy or blessed, and why?
3. When you think about the world as it should be, how hopeful are you? How do you define hope? How do you feel about Václav Havel's definition of hope?

15

The kingdom of God . . .

. . . is between the world as it is and the world as it should be.

Followers of Jesus are not hopeful in a blissfully ignorant sort of way. We don't pretend that the kingdom of God has arrived or even that we are doing a great job of bringing it about. To borrow a phrase from community organizing, we know that we exist in the world as it is and that the world is full of sin, which is the word we Christians use for human weakness and failings.

Right after we pray the Our Father, at the direction of Jesus, that God's kingdom come, (and that God's will be done) "on earth as it is in heaven," we pray, in effect, "And forgive us our weakness and failings, as we forgive the weakness and failings of others." We don't take a show of hands. We know that sin is part of daily life.

But we also know that sinfulness doesn't have to be the last word on the subject. The way we put it is that Jesus has saved the world from sin, that we have been redeemed from the world as it is by Jesus' life, death, and resurrection.

Part of this redemption involves us. For many years, Catholics and Protestants fought over faith versus works. Protestants emphasized that we were saved by faith alone, and Catholics insisted that faith always resulted in good works. A lot of this conflict came about because of the abuse of the Catholic doctrine of indulgences, which the Protestants saw as a way of buying your way out of sin and into heaven. But recently the Catholics and the Lutherans issued a joint statement in which they basically agreed that both faith and works are vital parts of Christian belief and practice.

The way St. James puts it in his single letter, which has a prominent position in the New Testament, right after the letters attributed to Paul and before even the letters of Peter and John: "Listen, dear friends. Isn't it clear by now that God operates quite differently? He chose the world's down-and-out as the kingdom's first citizens, with full rights and privileges. This kingdom is promised to anyone who loves God" (James 2:5, *The Message*).

James goes on to say, "You can no more show me your works apart from your faith than I can show you my faith apart from my works. Faith and works, works and faith, fit together hand in glove" (James 2:18, *The Message*).

For Christians, it is these works that help move the world from what it is to what it should be. If we were to deny that the world is not yet the kingdom of God, we would be both foolish and hypocritical—foolish because it is so obvious, and hypocritical because we would be telling people that there is nothing we can do about it, when we know there is.

This is what puts some Christians at the forefront of many efforts to make the world a better place. We recognize that the world is in need of redemption, even though we believe it has already been redeemed. We are right there on the cusp of the two worlds: having a vision of what the world could be but recognizing that it is not yet there.

There is a term that many groups, including Christians, use for this existence between the two worlds: *social justice*. Social justice is not merely fairness or honesty—we call that commutative justice. Nor is it charitable work—we call that distributive justice. Both of those kinds of justice are important, but social justice is the big enchilada of the kingdom of God.

Social justice recognizes the reality of inequalities and poverty and oppression; the world is sin-filled, we Christians would say. The good news is that, because of the teaching and example of Jesus, we now know what the world is supposed to be like, and we are committed to working to make it that way.

Social justice, however, gets us into very murky territory, precisely because it is about changing the basic structures and institutions of our society. It is much easier to be kind or honest or generous with others in our immediate circles of influence than it is to fight to make things right for everyone.

First of all, it is not always clear what is the right thing to do. Sometimes we think a particular reform of society is what is needed to make the world a better place, and we discover that—despite our best efforts—we often fail miserably. Changes we make backfire, or they have unintended consequences, or they eventually outlive their usefulness and become part of the problem. We recognize this, and it humbles us and makes us less self-righteous and more willing to listen to others and work with them on other possible ideas.

Second, social justice, while it strives to make the world as it should be, begins with the world as it is. That means that it is governed by the rules of this world, not the next world. Social justice leads us into the realms of politics, economics, business, law, and international relations—the realms of power and influence and money. Christians, like everyone else, cannot afford to be rigid and absolute. We have to work with others to come up with solutions, but we also have to exercise our own power to have our point of view heard in the mix. Social justice is the arena of compromise and the art of the possible. No social justice reform ever brings about the world as it should be completely and finally. It is either a step toward a better world or a step away from it.

So, Christians live with a foot in both worlds at all times. We keep the vision of the kingdom of God clearly in our sights. We also roll up our sleeves and deal with the realities of the way things are. If we focus too much on the world as it should be, we become inflexible and self-righteous. If we get stuck in the world as it is, we become cynical and manipulative.

It is in the space between the world as it is and the world as it should be that the kingdom of God begins.

Questions for Christians

1. Which side do you usually err on: the world as it is or the world as it should be? Explain.
2. How do you work for social justice in your life? What are the major problems or roadblocks you encounter?
3. Do you think that the world has been saved and redeemed? What does that mean to you? Why is there still sin in the world?

Questions for Dialogue with Non-Christians

1. What does sin or evil mean in your tradition? Where does it come from? How do you combat it?
2. Do you have a concept of social justice that is different from commutative or distributive justice? How do you speak of it? How do you try to bring social justice about?
3. Do the concepts of the world as it is and the world as it should be resonate with you? How? How do you operate in both worlds at the same time?

16

The kingdom of God . . .

. . . *is for the young and the young at heart.*

What are we to make of Jesus' repeated statement that if we don't become like little children, we can never enter the kingdom of God? The obvious answers are that we must have unwavering faith, that we must be pure of heart, that we must accept people for who they are, for this is the nature of children. And these are certainly attributes of the kingdom of God that Jesus envisioned.

But there is a deeper reason that the kingdom of God is for the young, and I become more aware of this reason the older I get (sixty-two and counting, thank you).

Perhaps the way to look at it is to consider who were the opposite of children, in Jesus' time and in ours. The people who really seemed to make Jesus mad, who simply couldn't get what he was talking about, were the scribes, the elders, the Pharisees, the Sadducees, the high priest of his own Jewish religion. What was it that bugged him about them? They were the adults, the ones who knew what was best for people, the ones who had it all figured out, the ones who had been there and done that and wanted to protect others (especially the young) from making any mistakes or trying anything new.

Sound familiar? Of course it is. It is how our parents were with us, and how we are—or will be—with our kids or grandkids. It is the nature of getting old to become more set in our ways, more aware of the dangers out there, less willing to try something we either have never tried before or—even worse—something that we tried once or twice that didn't work out.

Actually, the caution and conservatism of adults are healthy to a degree. They can prevent us from repeating our mistakes. There is something about adulthood, however, that apparently hinders a person trying to enter the kingdom of God, and perhaps it lies in the very nature of maturity.

By his words and his actions, Jesus seems to be saying that we should never be satisfied with the world as it is. We cannot be beaten down by the impossibility of the task or the strength of our opposition. We have to become more like little children, who think they can accomplish anything they want, rather than act like responsible adults, who *know* they cannot accomplish everything they want.

In literature, we have a great example of this in the book *Don Quixote* by Miguel Cervantes. What is the main character, Don Quixote, if not a child? He is out tilting at windmills, thinking his prostitute girlfriend is a great lady, and trying to make the world a better place against impossible odds. What do we adults do with such a character? We turn his last name into an adjective that is used almost exclusively with a negative connotation: *quixotic*, which means "idealistic," "visionary," "impractical," or "impracticable."

Well, what idea could possibly be more idealistic, visionary, impractical, or impracticable than trying to make this world more like the way God would have it, more like the way things are in heaven? So, it appears that the only way we will be able to sustain this mission is if we become like little children.

Jesus had a great sense of humor, something that shows in the Gospel stories, although it is somewhat obscured for us today by two thousand years of piety. Jesus' humor comes out especially when he is talking about the kingdom of God. He said that if we had faith in it, we could tell a mountain to move over there and it would. He challenged Peter, the ultimate adult in most of the Gospel stories, to walk on the water, and Peter did it for a few seconds, until his adult brain took over and he began to sink. Jesus ordered the disciples to feed thousands of people with a few loaves and fish. These scenes are funny, the kind of things a kid would come up with. But they make a greater point that only a child would believe, which is that nothing is impossible with God—not even the establishment of God's reign on earth.

Jesus' great debate with Nicodemus, a member of the Sanhedrin, the Jewish ruling council, is a stitch. Nicodemus is an adult, and therefore cannot get Jesus' idea of the kingdom of God. He comes to Jesus at night, probably because he is afraid of what other adults might think. Jesus takes his argument to the ultimate in childish imagination by telling Nicodemus that unless he is born again (or becomes a newborn baby), he can't be part of the kingdom of God. Nicodemus, sounding like the wise, educated, literal leader he was, replies, "How can these things be?" Jesus answers, "Are you a teacher of Israel, and yet you do not understand these things?" (John 3:9–10). You can almost see Jesus' sly smile as he delivers that line.

Then Jesus goes on to say what are arguably the most famous two verses in the Christian Scriptures: "This is how much God loved the world: He gave his Son, his one and only Son. And this is why: so that no one need be destroyed; by believing in him, anyone can have a whole and lasting life. God didn't go to all the trouble of sending his Son merely to point an accusing finger, telling the world how bad it was. He came to help, to put the world right again" (John 3:16–17, *The Message*).

Here's the good news for Nicodemus and the rest of us oldsters: the kingdom of God is not just for the young; it is also for the young at heart. Nicodemus apparently finally got it at the end, when he somehow summoned enough courage to help bury Jesus' body, and tradition puts him among the leaders of the early church. Many of our best saints were very childlike, including Francis of Assisi, Mother Teresa, and Thérèse of Lisieux. More important, we all know older people who somehow maintain their childlike spirit of joy and optimism right up to the very end of their earthly life. For an example, watch the great documentary film, *Young@Heart*. Those are people who truly have been born again.

In the end, the kingdom of God is for the young and the young at heart. It is for our young adult children and eventually for their children and their children's children. But it is also for anyone who can become like a child. The young and the young at heart are the only ones who will have the faith and the courage to "dream the impossible dream" as Quixote did in the musical *The Man of La Mancha*—and as Jesus certainly did.

Questions for Christians

1. Where are you on the young-old continuum spiritually and emotionally? What percentage of you is young, and what percentage is old? Explain why.
2. What is your impression of Jesus' sense of humor or lack of it. Give an example or two to support your ideas.
3. What does it mean to you that the kingdom of God is for the young and the young at heart?

Questions for Dialogue with Non-Christians

1. How are children viewed in your tradition?
2. What are the spiritual and emotional traits your tradition promotes or celebrates for those trying to make the world a better place? How many of them could be described as childlike?
3. What role, if any, does humor play in your tradition? What are some examples?

The kingdom of God . . .

. . . is not just for Christians.

Reverend Paul Brian Campbell, SJ, uses his experience at the Shrine of Our Lady of Lourdes in France to describe the Christian idea of the kingdom of God. "When you actually get to the center of the shrine," he says, "after you've walked past all the peripheral touristy stuff, you look around and you suddenly realize that everything has been turned on its head. For at Lourdes, it is the disabled and the sick and the sick-at-heart who are important. They are first in line. They are the reason the place exists. The rest of us, who are of able body and soul, are there to support them."

"That," says Father Campbell, "is the Christian view of the kingdom of God. Everything is upside down."

The kingdom of God is not just for Christians. It is good news for everyone, if they choose to participate in it, and even if they don't, because ultimately everyone benefits when the world is turned on its head.

This is one of the main problems with equating the kingdom of God with a reward after death, which many Christians and non-Christians do. If the kingdom is a reward-punishment system for the next life, then it leads to all kinds of intellectual debate about who is going to be in and who is going to be out. We must confess that the Christian churches of all denominations have bought into this view over the centuries. It was—and continues to be—a way to keep the faithful in line in terms of moral rules and religious practice. Also, this view of the kingdom of God creates an exclusive system: "I'm saved; I'm going to heaven; I'm a member of the one true church; and so-and-so is not."

Some of the apocalyptic and end-of-times stories in the Scriptures appear to reinforce this view. The wheat and the chaff are going to be separated, with the chaff thrown into the fire. Some people are welcome at the banquet of the king, while others are thrown out where there is "weeping and gnashing of teeth" (Matthew 22:13). Jesus says, "Very truly, I tell you, no one can enter the kingdom of God without being born of water and Spirit" (John 3:5).

So, why isn't the kingdom of God exclusively for Christians? Well, perhaps it is—but only as a metaphor. By this I mean that "the kingdom of God" is a particular way of talking about the world as it should be, a metaphor presented to us by Jesus that we his followers try to use, as Father Campbell did in describing his experience at Lourdes. But that metaphor is not supposed to imply that the kingdom of God is an exclusionary club designed to put down others or stake some claim to moral or spiritual superiority. "The kingdom of God" is merely the Christian phrase for a world where God's will is done, on earth as it is in heaven.

Can non-Christians share this view of the world as it should be? Of course they can, and many do. Is it right for Christians to force others to share our religious language and preferences to work with us to fulfill this vision? Obviously not. In the Gospel of Mark, Jesus put it this way when faced with someone who was doing good but was not part of his group of followers: "Whoever is not against us is for us" (Mark 9:40; see Luke 9:50). That's a pretty good prescription for how we Christians should handle our efforts to include others in helping to bring about the kingdom of God.

Will everyone else share our view on everything? No. Some elements of the Christian view are so radical and out of the mainstream that we cannot possibly expect all people to embrace them. That might happen, but only after a long period of showing by example that the law of love would work in a particular situation. The abortion issue may be a contemporary example of this. Unless and until those of us who are pro-life demonstrate that we support life in every conceivable situation, we will not succeed in promoting our views on the sanctity of life in the womb.

There is a lot of room for compromise with and even incorporation of the views of others into our vision of the world as it should be. Christians have to keep in mind that our beliefs and values don't come whole or all at once even to us. For example, many Christians were initially not opposed to slavery or in favor of women's suffrage. Eventually, though, we came to see freedom and equality as part of the way the world should be for all humans. Today, many Christians are now struggling with how to extend the rights to freedom and equality to our gay and lesbian brothers and sisters.

So, Christians do not have exclusive ownership of the world-as-it-should-be vision. We do, however, have a compelling vision, parts of which many others share, even if they do not use our words for it. They have their own words, and we need to understand them as well. That is one reason the kingdom of God is not just for Christians.

When God's kingdom truly becomes present in this world, everyone will benefit. Of this there can be no doubt. In fact, any scenario in which some people (or Christians only) reap the benefits while others are left out cannot be the kingdom described by Jesus of Nazareth. He apparently came to understand that his vision of the kingdom of God was not just for the Jews but for all people. In this he was schooled by a Gentile woman who confronted him on the issue and convinced him that she was as worthy of the benefits of his newly launched kingdom as anyone else: "Sir, even the dogs under the table eat the children's crumbs" (Mark 7:28).

The kingdom of God is, literally, for everyone. People can, of course, choose not to participate in it, and many have—including large numbers of Christians. But where the kingdom of God breaks out, it breaks out for all. It is the way the world should be, the way God would have it.

Questions for Christians

1. Have you been conditioned or taught to believe that you have proprietary rights concerning the kingdom of God? In other words, do you feel that, because you are Christian, you have a special place in the kingdom? If so, please elaborate. If not, explain why.
2. Why does the kingdom of God have to be for everyone? What would it mean if it were not?
3. When, if ever, are you tempted to impose your Christian view on others? When you witness the Christian view being pushed in a situation, what do you see as the results?

Questions for Dialogue with Non-Christians

1. What elements of the Christian view of the kingdom of God might your tradition embrace? Which ones would it reject, and why?

2. Is there any history of religious or moral judgment or triumphalism in your tradition? Can you describe it? How is that viewed now?

3. Does your tradition view compromise as a strength or as a weakness? What are some examples?

18

The kingdom of God . . .

. . . *is not for everyone.*

Many Christians, while talking enthusiastically about the kingdom of God, mostly as heaven or as the life to come, don't actually live out Jesus' vision as a functional plan for their daily actions or their view of how the world should be. Their basic attitude is that this is impossible for ordinary people: "Well, of course Jesus could live that way, but he couldn't possibly have expected the rest of us to do that. The world simply could not function solely on the law of love."

Likewise, many non-Christians balk at Jesus' vision for the world. Although they may admire much about him and his teaching, they find it impossible to give him the last word on how the world should be. Their basic attitude might be summarized this way: "Well, Jesus had a lot of good things to say, but we certainly can't embrace his idea of the kingdom of God as a direct revelation from God. There are too many pieces of it that are impractical or impossible to put into action."

Jesus seemed to be pretty accepting of both these responses. It appears he never expected everyone to believe him or accept his vision for the world. He said, "For many are called, but few are chosen" (Matthew 22:14), and "The harvest is plentiful, but the laborers are few" (Luke 10:2).

In one delicious turn in the New Testament, Jesus appears to have answered the same question two different ways, concerning people's participation in the kingdom. In Mark 9:40 (see Luke 9:50), he says, "Whoever is not against us is for us," and in Matthew 12:30 and Luke 11:23 he says, "Whoever is not with me is against me." So much for using a single text of Scripture to prove a point!

What we can learn from these two diametrically opposed statements is that Jesus and his followers were clear that people would have mixed responses to the kingdom of God. Some would want to be involved in bringing about the kingdom, even if they would not join the group or use the phrase. Others would actively oppose them. Still others would say they were for the kingdom of God, but they wouldn't do much to bring it about. The author of the book of Revelation was especially disgusted with this last group, saying, "So, because you are lukewarm, and neither cold nor hot, I am about to spit you out of my mouth" (Revelation 3:16).

The early Christians must have recognized that theirs was a pretty radical view of the world as it should be and therefore would never be for everyone. Just look at the way Jesus' story ended. It is clear that something in his teaching about the kingdom of God threatened both the civil and the religious authorities of the time—so much so that they put him to death in the most shameful way they knew. For them, this was the end of the story, as it was for many of Jesus' followers. In their world, nothing was worse than a crucifixion; it meant a complete loss of dignity and power. It was the ultimate humiliation, proof that you must have done something terribly wrong to deserve it.

St. Paul said that the crucifixion was the main reason the fledgling Christian movement was not for everyone. He said that the crucified Christ was "a stumbling-block to Jews and foolishness to Gentiles" (1 Corinthians 1:23). In purely human terms, Jesus' view of the kingdom of God is a nonstarter. It is obvious to us that we could never operate society by the principles he espoused. They will never work. What's worse, if we attempt to implement them, not only will we fail but also we might end up like Jesus himself: scorned and ridiculed by the powers that be and failing utterly to bring about the better world we say we want.

That is where the Christian belief in the resurrection of Jesus comes in. As Paul says, if the Resurrection didn't happen, then we Christians most certainly are fools: "If Christ has not been raised, then our proclamation has been in vain and your faith has been in vain" (1 Corinthians 15:14). Because of the Resurrection, Christians believe that anything is possible, including living authentically in the here-and-now kingdom of God.

But the Resurrection is for believers only. Even the disciples couldn't believe their own eyes. The Resurrection stories in the Gospels are among the most contradictory and difficult to understand in all of Scripture: Who saw Jesus first? Did they recognize him or not? Did he have a body like ours, or could he walk through walls? Did he ascend to heaven or did he go before them into Galilee? There is not one historical reference to anyone who was not a follower of Jesus ever seeing him alive after he had died. He was apparently seen only through the eyes of faith. Faith in what? Faith in Jesus' vision of the kingdom of God for this world: "After his suffering, he presented himself alive to them by many convincing proofs, appearing to them during forty days and speaking about the kingdom of God" (Acts 1:3).

Here's the point: It doesn't matter what the exact details of the Resurrection were. Paul, who was probably the one most responsible for the spread of Christianity, wasn't present during the events of the Resurrection, the Ascension, and Pentecost. He encountered the living Jesus years later on the road to Damascus, where he was going to persecute the very ones who believed that Jesus had risen. Jesus himself had told Thomas, "Blessed are those who have not seen and yet have come to believe" (John 20:29).

What are we to make of all this today? The lesson is that only those of us who can believe in the Resurrection can really believe in the kingdom of God. Otherwise, it is impossible. The kingdom of God is an impossible dream; but so is the Resurrection. For Christians the Resurrection means that God is faithful and ultimately in charge, that the just and the innocent will triumph in the end, and that the kingdom of God—as impractical as it seems as a way of organizing human behavior—will somehow be established in this world.

That is why the kingdom of God is not for everyone. It takes a leap of faith that many people—Christians and non-Christians alike—cannot make. We shouldn't be surprised by this. We shouldn't even be upset about it. On every rational level, others are right: the world cannot be run the way God would have it, any more than an innocent man who had been crucified on a cross could rise from the dead after three days. Only those of us who believe in Jesus of Nazareth could possibly think so.

Questions for Christians

1. What connections do you make between the Resurrection and the kingdom of God? If Jesus rose from the dead, what are the implications for how you live your life?
2. Why is the kingdom of God not for everyone? What are some examples of people you know who just can't buy it?
3. How and where do you encounter Jesus in your life? Could those moments be described as the kingdom of God?

Questions for Dialogue with Non-Christians

1. Do you consider the Christian belief in the Resurrection a stumbling block or foolishness? Please explain.
2. Which elements of the Christian vision of the kingdom of God are appealing to you? Which ones do you consider naive or impractical? Which ones do you consider wrong?
3. Which parts of your tradition are misunderstood, misinterpreted, or difficult to accept among those who are not members—or even some of those who are? Why do you believe them? What are the implications of those beliefs?

The kingdom of God . . .

. . . is first.

F or the Christian, the kingdom of God is supposed to come before everything else: politics, family, business, even religion. How realistic is this? In the world as it is, we've got bills to pay, children to raise, an environment to save, a president or governor or mayor to elect—not to mention cheering the Cubs on to their first World Series in more than a hundred years.

How could Jesus expect us to keep his vision for the world front and center at all times? Isn't this just hyperbole? Apparently not:

> On the road, someone asked Jesus if he could go along. "I'll go with you wherever," he said.
>
> Jesus was curt: "Are you ready to rough it? We're not staying in the best inns, you know."
>
> Jesus said to another, "Follow me."
>
> He said, "Certainly, but first excuse me for a couple of days, please. I have to make arrangements for my father's funeral."
>
> Jesus refused. "First things first. Your business is life, not death. And life is urgent: Announce God's kingdom!"
>
> Then another said, "I'm ready to follow you, Master, but first excuse me while I get things straightened out at home."

> Jesus said, "No procrastination. No backward looks. You
> can't put God's kingdom off till tomorrow. Seize the day."
>
> LUKE 9:57–62, *THE MESSAGE*

Actually, the New Testament is filled with statements like these that imply that for followers of Jesus normal life takes a backseat to faith life. In fact, these passages have been used for centuries to promote all kinds of religious rigor—celibacy, asceticism, vocations to the religious life.

This interpretation is partly because of the belief of many of the early Christians that the kingdom of God would soon come in its fullness—as evidenced by Christ's second coming—most likely in their own lifetimes. They didn't need to worry about mundane things such as jobs and mortgages and school tuitions. When this second coming of Christ didn't materialize as they expected, some turned their attention to the next life, life after death, as being what was really important.

Neither of these interpretations fits how Jesus himself saw the kingdom of God. For him, the kingdom had already begun. And it was a vision aimed at this world, not the next. So what might he have meant when he said, "But strive first for the kingdom of God and his righteousness, and all these things will be given to you as well" (Matthew 6:33)?

The first thing might be that we humans have to have a world as it should be. If we lose sight of what we are striving for, then we can never get there. In fact, if we don't remember where we want to go, we will make lots of mistakes and wrong turns because we will be making judgments on the basis of a vision other than the one we should be striving for.

Here's a small personal example. I coached kids' baseball for about ten years, when my kids were young. I did so because I love the game and wanted a way to relate to my three children. But I also did it because I observed how awful some coaches were; they may have been effective at teaching the skills of the game but not at teaching the kids good sportsmanship and life skills.

So, I had a vision of how I thought kids' baseball should be run. Whenever I kept that vision in front of me, I was a great coach. If I lost that vision, even for a moment, I would do things that were antithetical to how I thought coaches—and kids—ought to act.

I could give similar personal examples from marriage, parenting, business, civic affairs, even church. I'm sure you could do the same. What Jesus meant by his insistence that we put first the kingdom of God in our lives is that we always keep foremost in our minds his idea of how the world should be, so that all the actions and decisions we make are in line with that vision.

Jesus certainly wants us to bury our loved ones and make sure our affairs are in order. What he insists on, however, is that we never lose sight of the big picture, the kingdom of God. If we want to be a good kids' baseball coach, we have to remember why we became a coach in the first place; and if we want to enter the kingdom of God, then we have to keep that kingdom in mind at all times.

The other thing Jesus meant with his "strive first" demand has to do with religious belief and practice. For many Christians, as it is for many followers of other traditions, orthodoxy and piety are the highest values. Thus, there are people who feel that they are holy because they pray or go to church regularly or because they believe every doctrine to the letter.

If you put the kingdom first, however, then by definition it comes before even these things. That is not to say that the believers in the kingdom of God are not devout or faithful. It means that they do not allow devotions or doctrine to become more important than working for the kingdom.

There are lots of stories in the Gospels about this. Jesus does not allow the Sabbath to prevent him from curing people or the disciples from picking and eating grain. When someone is doing good in his name, Jesus does not tell him to stop, even if the person is not one of his followers. "Whoever is not against you is for you" (Luke 9:50; see Mark 9:40), he said. Another time he said, "Whoever is not with me is against me"" (Matthew 12:30; Luke 11:23). He might have added, "No matter how pious or doctrinally pure they are."

For Jesus, true holiness came from keeping his vision of the kingdom of God front and center. At one point, a woman shouted to him, "Blessed the womb that carried you, and the breasts at which you nursed!" But Jesus replied, "Even more blessed are those who hear God's Word and guard it with their lives!" (Luke 11:27–28, *The Message*).

Keeping the kingdom of God first is not about obsessing over your place in heaven. It is about making a vision of the world as it should be the basis for all your decisions in this life.

Questions for Christians

1. Describe an area or activity in your life in which you are fine when you keep your deepest convictions in mind but get into trouble when you lose sight of them. What happens in those situations?

2. Which comes first in your life: piety, orthodoxy, or the kingdom of God? Explain your answer. If you object to the question, why?

3. If you put the kingdom of God first at all times, how would that affect your normal life in the world as it is?

Questions for Dialogue with Non-Christians

1. What is the single most important thing in your tradition? Is it easy or difficult to maintain focus on it at all times in your own life? What are some examples?
2. Where do piety, devotion, contemplation, fidelity to rules or teachings, and action to improve the world rank in your tradition? Can you elaborate?
3. Do most Christians, in your experience, keep the kingdom of God first in their lives? Can you give some examples?

20

The kingdom of God . . .

. . . is a different way of seeing.

Some Buddhists recite this proverb: "Before I was enlightened, I chopped wood and carried water. After I was enlightened, I chopped wood and carried water."

Christians who believe in the kingdom of God understand this statement, for it is very much like the way Jesus described his idea of the kingdom of God. When it came to his vision for the world, Jesus was often enigmatic, using parables and similes to try to get his point across. Near the beginning of the very first Gospel written, Jesus says, "With what can we compare the kingdom of God, or what parable will we use for it?" (Mark 4:30). He then went on to compare the kingdom of God to a mustard seed, "which, when sown upon the ground, is the smallest of all the seeds on earth; yet when it is sown it grows up and becomes the greatest of all shrubs, and puts forth large branches, so that the birds of the air can make nests in its shade" (Mark 4:31–32).

That's it. No further explanation. Jesus is not trying to give an exact description of the kingdom of God, much less a set of directions. A little earlier in the same Gospel, Jesus implies that he doesn't even care if everyone understands what he is talking about. He explains to his disciples:

> You've been given insight into God's kingdom—you know how it works. But to those who can't see it yet, everything comes in stories, creating readiness, nudging them toward receptive insight. These are people—
>> Whose eyes are open but don't see a thing,
>> Whose ears are open but don't understand a word,
>> Who avoid making an about-face and getting forgiven.
>
> MARK 4:11–12, *THE MESSAGE*

This seems fairly harsh coming from someone as loving and optimistic as Jesus, but apparently there is something about spiritual sight that is the key to the kingdom, and apparently not even Jesus could force people to see in this way. Many of his stories and even some of his miracles were about seeing things in a different way. For example, in the Gospel of Mark, Jesus heals a blind man at Bethsaida. Jesus lays his hands on the man and then asks if he can see anything. "I can see people, but they look like trees, walking" (Mark 8:24). Then Jesus lays his hands on the man again and he sees everything perfectly.

In the Gospel of John one of the main signs of the coming of the kingdom that Jesus performed was healing a man who had been blind from birth. It was quite an extended drama, one the church uses each year around Easter to explain the central themes of the kingdom (see John 9:1–41).

First of all, the blind man is brought to Jesus' attention by his disciples, who want to know whether it was the man himself or his parents who had sinned badly enough to cause his blindness. This is a fundamental error in people's perceptions of God's ways, and Jesus set about correcting the popular misconception that bad things are a punishment from God (which many people, including Christians, still hold).

> Jesus said, "You're asking the wrong question. You're looking for someone to blame. There is no such cause-effect here. Look instead for what God can do. We need to be energetically at work for the One who sent me here, working while the sun shines. When night falls, the workday is over. For as long as I am in the world, there is plenty of light. I am the world's Light."
>
> JOHN 9:3–5, *THE MESSAGE*

So, Jesus goes to work, making some mud with his spit, putting it on the man's eyes, and telling him to go wash in the pool of Siloam (which means "sent"). The man does so and comes back able to see. Now the story really gets interesting.

First of all, there is some question about whether they've got the right man. Could this really be the man born blind? Nobody who is born blind ever gets to see, so maybe they have the man mixed up with someone else. To paraphrase, the man says, "Nope, it's me all right." He tells them what happened and that it was Jesus who did this for him, but when they ask him where Jesus is, he says, "I don't have the slightest idea."

Then the religious leaders of the time get involved. They start questioning the man. What really has them upset is not that he can see but that he has been cured on the Sabbath, which means that Jesus has broken the religious law. So, they start grilling the poor guy who has just been cured. (So much for allowing him any time to absorb this miracle and celebrate it!) At first, he's not quite sure what has happened to him or why, but he never wavers from his basic story: he was born blind, Jesus cured him, and now he can see. The leaders even call in the man's parents, but they refuse to get involved because it has already been decided that anyone who confesses Jesus as the Messiah will be put out of the synagogue. They do, however, confirm that this is their son and that he has been blind from birth.

They call in the man a second time, and this time he is more assertive:

> "I've told you over and over and you haven't listened. Why do you want to hear it again? Are you so eager to become his disciples?"
>
> With that they jumped all over him. "You might be a disciple of that man, but we're disciples of Moses. We know for sure that God spoke to Moses, but we have no idea where this man even comes from."
>
> The man replied: "This is amazing! You claim to know nothing about him, but the fact is, he opened my eyes! It's well known that God isn't at the beck and call of sinners, but listens carefully to anyone who lives in reverence and does his will. That someone opened the eyes of a man born blind has never been heard of—ever. If this man didn't come from God, he wouldn't be able to do anything."
>
> JOHN 9:27–33, *THE MESSAGE*

They throw the man out, but Jesus finds him and says, "I came into the world to bring everything into the clear light of day, making all the distinctions clear, so that those who have never seen will see, and those who have made a great pretense of seeing will be exposed as blind" (John 9:39, *The Message*).

The religious leaders overhear this and say, "Does that mean you're calling us blind?" Jesus replies, "If you were really blind, you would be blameless, but since you claim to see everything so well, you're accountable for every fault and failure" (John 9:40–41, *The Message*).

Jesus was trying to change how we see the world and its possibilities. Apparently this vision is not a matter of intellectual knowledge or understanding. It's a matter of the heart and the senses.

Questions for Christians

1. What does it mean to really see something? From your own life, what is an example of a time when you finally saw something clearly that you had not seen before?
2. Why do you think Jesus was so enigmatic in his descriptions of the kingdom of God?
3. Which of Jesus' parables of the kingdom of God best help you see what he was talking about? Why?

Questions for Dialogue with Non-Christians

1. How is the metaphor of seeing or regaining sight used in your tradition? What are some examples?
2. Have leaders in your tradition ever gotten in the way of new insights?
3. Do any of Jesus' parables of the kingdom of God best help you see what he was talking about? If so, which ones and why?

The kingdom of God . . .

. . . *is not fair.*

I desire mercy and not sacrifice" (Matthew 12:7, see Hosea 6:6).
If it's fairness you want, the kingdom of God is not for you.
If it's mercy you desire (as Jesus quoted the prophet Hosea), then
it may be.

The kingdom of God is not an economic system like, say, capi-
talism or socialism. Had Jesus been around today, he would have
been challenging economists to use their knowledge to help create
the common good. Jesus saw no problems in getting everyone
into the kingdom. To him, everything was possible. He left us to
worry about the details.

What Jesus did not worry about is what we call fairness. He
was on the side of the poor and oppressed, and he wanted them
out of their poverty and oppression. When he healed people, he
was an equal-opportunity miracle worker. It didn't matter to him
whether the person was the son of a Roman official or a blind man
so isolated from others that no one would help him into a pool
to be healed. Jesus cured them both, just because he was asked.
If five thousand people were hungry, Jesus would tell his disciples
to feed them all. He didn't worry about who was responsible and

who was irresponsible about bringing food with them to his rallies. If people were hungry, Jesus was going to feed them, and to hell with fairness.

When the disciples started wondering what payoff they'd receive for all the sacrifices they were making to follow Jesus (that is, demanding a just wage for their work), Jesus promised them that they would get paid for their efforts. The pay, however, would include suffering and persecution. "Mark my words, no one who sacrifices house, brothers, sisters, mother, father, children, land—whatever—because of me and the Message will lose out. They'll get it all back, but multiplied many times in homes, brothers, sisters, mothers, children, and land—but also in troubles. And then the bonus of eternal life!" (Mark 10:29–30, *The Message*). Yet the poor disciples couldn't even count on being first in line: "This is once again the Great Reversal: Many who are first will end up last, and the last first" (Mark 10:31, *The Message*). How's that for basic unfairness?

The reason Jesus could be so oblivious to the practicalities of the situation is that he did not see scarcity. He saw abundance. If the disciples could scrounge up only a few loaves and a couple of pieces of fish, that was enough for Jesus. And somehow he was right, to the point that they had more left over than they started with. This is Kingdom Economics 101: there is more than enough for everyone.

Jesus took this view of the world as it should be to ridiculous lengths, to points where none of us would ever go. He told a parable about a group of unemployed people who were hanging around one morning doing nothing. Doing nothing in the kingdom of God is not a good thing. Jesus' God wants everyone to be fruitful (see Matthew 20:1–16).

In the story, let's make it a businesswoman who sees the people doing nothing and hires them to go and work for her company. She comes back at noon and finds more people not working and hires them as well. The same thing happens at three in the afternoon. Finally, she finds more people idle at five o'clock and hires them, too—right before closing time.

When it comes time to pay the people, she starts with the people who came last and gives them a full day's wage. "Hot dog!" the others think. "We've hit a bleeding-heart liberal today. Surely all of us will receive a fat bonus."

But the businesswoman pays everyone the same wage, even those who worked the entire day. "That's not fair," the early-bird workers complain. "We busted our butts all day, and we get paid the same as these slackers who worked less than an hour."

The businesswoman says to them, "Hey, I contracted with you for a day's wage, and that's what I paid you. If I choose to pay these others more, it's my money, isn't it? Are you jealous because I'm generous?"

Are you jealous because I am generous? Of course we are. We like fairness in our economic system, not generosity. Otherwise, how will we know who the winners and losers are? How will we ever motivate people to work hard? We don't mind equality of opportunity, but equality of result? That seems totally unfair.

It *is* unfair. That's why Jesus was not an economist. He didn't have to worry about gross national products and inflation and depression and all the things we have to worry about in the world as it is. He was talking about the world as it should be, and in that world, nobody is left behind and everyone has what they need to survive and thrive.

How do we possibly get to the world as it should be? Maybe we don't. Maybe the kingdom never comes, or never comes completely, in this world. Maybe we always exist in the space between the world as it is and the world as it should be.

But that doesn't mean we have to make an idol out of fairness. Perhaps fairness is overrated—it certainly isn't a top priority in the kingdom of God. This was best explained to me by a Catholic priest, Father William Burke, who once said about this story: "The key to the parable of the workers hired at different times is simple: We were all hired at five o'clock!"

Questions for Christians

1. What does it mean that "we were all hired at five o'clock"? How does that change the way you look at the issue of fairness?
2. What are the practical problems with generosity? How does abundance affect those problems?
3. Could the world ever really function according to Jesus' view of things? If not, does that negate the value of his vision? Explain.

Questions for Dialogue with Non-Christians

1. How does the modern discipline of economics fit in with your tradition's view of the world as it should be?
2. What is your tradition's view of the difference between fairness and generosity?
3. Is your tradition ever impractical in its beliefs and teachings? What are some examples?

22

The kingdom of God . . .

. . . *is not coercive.*

Many people of diverse ideologies have a vision of the world as it should be, and some of them are so convinced and committed to their beliefs that they are willing to force other people to adopt them. This is true, of course, in politics, where much of history has been about one country or group trying to impose its will on another. It is also true of much religious history, including that of Christianity.

If you go back to what Jesus said, and especially to how he acted, it is clear that his idea of the kingdom of God was not coercive. Certainly there were passages in which he seemed to say that there was going to be a judgment in which the good people would be rewarded and the bad people would be punished. But these were always based on choices the people themselves had made (see Matthew 25:31–46). They either helped the poor and visited the sick and imprisoned and clothed the naked and fed the hungry, or they didn't. In either case, they brought judgment on themselves by how they acted or failed to act.

But Jesus was against forcing a person's will. Everyone was free to make his or her own decisions about the kingdom of God, from Judas Iscariot to Pontius Pilate to the woman caught in adultery. If people did not choose to participate in the kingdom, Jesus was sad. He wept over Jerusalem; he predicted that Peter would deny him three times. Still, he never resorted to forcing anyone to follow him.

The Gospel of Luke presents the story of a rich official who comes to Jesus and asks what he must do to enter the kingdom of God. Jesus tells him to obey the Ten Commandments. The man says he has done so since his youth. Jesus tells him there is only one thing left to do: "Sell everything you own and give it away to the poor. You will have riches in heaven. Then come, follow me." Luke says, "This was the last thing the official expected to hear. He was very rich and became terribly sad. He was holding on tight to a lot of things and not about to let them go" (Luke 18:22–23, *The Message*).

Jesus does not try to dissuade the man, much less coerce him. He merely points out to his disciples how difficult it is for most people of means to enter into the kingdom of God. Here he uses the famous metaphor that it is easier to thread a camel through the eye of a needle than for a rich person to enter the kingdom. His disciples asked him who had any chance at all of entering the kingdom, and Jesus answered that there was no chance "if you think you can pull it off by yourself. Every chance in the world if you trust God to do it" (Luke 18:27, *The Message*).

So, there is no hint of coercion in Jesus' approach. He genuinely wants people to choose the kingdom of God, but he is not naive about the difficulty in doing so.

Jesus' entire life is played out this way. His is an offer, not a demand. When he engages a Samaritan woman in conversation at a well (see John 4:1–42), he doesn't try to scare her into believing in him or his message. He merely promises "living water" that never needs to be replenished. The woman is free to choose it or not. She does choose it, which leads Jesus to tell his disciples, "I'm telling you to open your eyes and take a good look at what's right in front of you. These Samaritan fields are ripe. It's harvest time!" (John 4:35, *The Message*).

Even during his trial, torture, and execution, Jesus never plays the coercion card. When Jesus is arrested, Peter draws a sword and cuts off the ear of Malchus, a servant of the high priest. Jesus orders Peter to put down his sword, and tradition has it that he healed Malchus's ear. Jesus might want Malchus to join the kingdom of God, but he wants him to do so only voluntarily.

At Jesus' civil trial, Pilate asks him if he is king of the Jews. "My kingdom," Jesus tells him, "doesn't consist of what you see around you. If it did, my followers would fight so that I wouldn't be handed over to the Jews. But I'm not that kind of king, not the world's kind of king" (John 18:36, *The Message*).

"So, are you a king or not?" Pilate asks again. "You tell me," Jesus responds. "Because I am King, I was born and entered the world so that I could witness to the truth. Everyone who cares for truth, who has any feeling for the truth, recognizes my voice" (John 18:37, *The Message*).

In other words, Jesus is willing to allow his vision of the world as it should be to speak for itself. If he is telling the truth (which he firmly believes he is), then those who are looking for the truth will recognize it in what he says. There is no need to force others to do so. They'll never get it anyway, unless they have a change of heart.

This great insight into Jesus' concept of the kingdom of God ends on the cross. There he is faithful to his understanding of God and what God wants for this world. He refuses to fight back, to condemn his enemies, to force anyone to stick with him, to curse God and die. There is a touching scene at the cross where Jesus is hung between two criminals (in the Gospel of Matthew they are called "revolutionaries"). The one thief chimes in with the crowd and mocks Jesus for not being able to save himself and them.

The other thief, however, accepts the invitation to join the kingdom of God at the last possible second. "Jesus, remember me when you come into your kingdom," he says. Jesus answers him, "Truly I tell you, today you will be with me in Paradise" (Luke 23:42–43).

You can't make anyone join the kingdom of God. But anyone who wants to is welcome, whenever he or she is ready. We Christians are not supposed to impose on others our ideas about the world as it should be, but neither are we to become reticent, afraid to speak up about the kingdom. The world as it should be is an offer that can be chosen only freely.

Questions for Christians

1. If the kingdom of God is the right plan for the world, why can't we force people to accept it?
2. How do we share our vision of the world as it should be with others in effective ways? What are some examples?
3. Imagine that in the conversation between Pilate and Jesus, Pilate comes to the same conclusion as the good thief. What would Pilate have said and done?

Questions for Dialogue with Non-Christians

1. How does your tradition define truth? How do you come to recognize what is true and what is false?

2. St. Paul says that the cross is a stumbling block for some and folly for others. What do you think of Jesus' death by crucifixion? Does it prevent you from believing his vision of how the world should be, or does his martyrdom lend credibility to his claims?

3. What part, if any, has coercion played in the history of your faith tradition? What is your opinion of religious coercion, and why?

The kingdom of God . . .

. . . *is the law of love.*

I f Christians were to give a one-sentence description of the world as it should be, it would be this: "The world is at its best when it is powered and organized by the law of love."

Love is often a "soft" word. Love offers images of flowers and candy on Valentine's Day; we love our favorite sports team; we fall in love (and out of love); we "love the one we're with," "make love, not war," and "love to love ya, baby."

Worse than softness, however, is how we humans can twist the truth about love. We cut people out of our lives; we wage war; we pollute the environment; we cheat, lie, and steal—all the while convincing ourselves that it is the loving thing to do, or at least that we have no choice. We call it self-preservation or self-interest, or we say that we are practicing tough love.

Jesus, of course, would have none of this. His idea of love was quite clear: we are sons and daughters of God, and therefore we should act as God does. How does God act? According to St. John's first letter:

God is love. When we take up permanent residence in a life of love, we live in God and God lives in us. This way, love has the run of the house, becomes at home and mature in us, so that we're free of worry on Judgment Day—our standing in the world is identical with Christ's. There is no room in love for fear. Well-formed love banishes fear. Since fear is crippling, a fearful life—fear of death, fear of judgment—is one not yet fully formed in love.

1 JOHN 4:17–18, *The Message*

Do Christians really believe that in the world as it should be everyone would live in perfect harmony? Well, most of us do believe it's like that in heaven, in some way that we really don't understand. And if we think we are trying to make things on earth as they are "in heaven," then maybe we do believe that humans are capable of building a world powered and organized by the law of love.

More likely, however, we see the law of love as a goal, something we strive for but fail to accomplish regularly. To that extent, we Christians live in the world as it is along with everyone else. We even have a word for our failure to love. We call it *sin* and acknowledge that we are all sinners.

But we do believe that Jesus is "the way, and the truth, and the life" (John 14:6), and so we try to follow his law of love, even when we don't understand how it could possibly be practical. Jesus promised:

Believe me: I am in my Father and my Father is in me. If you can't believe that, believe what you see—these works. The person who trusts me will not only do what I'm doing but even greater things, because I, on my way to the Father, am giving you the same work to do that I've been doing. You can count on it.

JOHN 14:11–12, *The Message*

We Christians believe in the kingdom of God because we have observed and experienced little pockets of it. We have seen people—ourselves and others—act in ways that can only be described as loving, and we say to ourselves, "What if the world could always be like that?" We call that vision the kingdom of God.

Do we believe the human race will ever get there? On our best days we do. We see progress in many areas, we see people change their ways, we have hope that the next generation will do a better job than we did. We see diseases that have been controlled, whole countries that live in peace, societies that have lifted most people out of poverty and educated their entire population.

But there is still so much incomprehensible evil in the world: terrorism, war, genocide, financial collapse, homelessness, mass unemployment. How can people be so hate filled, so violent, so cynical, so selfish? It's hard to see how we could ever get to the point at which everyone would live by the law of love.

Our answer is faith. We believe it because we have seen it, and we have seen it because Jesus showed it to us.

So, for the Christian, the law of love is something that is already here but is always on the way. We don't get caught up in the what-ifs of how it would all work out. We merely say, "That is where we want to go. We know it is the right way. We have seen it work many times in society and in our own lives. We aren't going to force people to follow the law of love, we are merely going to encourage them to change their hearts and give it a try. If enough people do so, God's kingdom will come."

Will there be laws in the world as it should be? Probably, but most, if not all, people will agree with them and follow them willingly. Will there be wars, poverty, starvation, disease? Probably not, or at least they will be eradicated quickly by the concerted effort of everyone. Will people actually love one another the way Christ loved us? Apparently so. Do we expect the kingdom of God to arrive soon? We don't have the slightest idea. We know neither the day nor the hour, and neither did Jesus.

All we Christians know is that the law of love is God's plan for the world, that it has already begun in our own lives and in the lives of others, and that eventually it will be in effect "on earth as it is in heaven."

That is enough for us.

Questions for Christians

1. Tell about a time when you followed the law of love. What happened?
2. Could an entire society or the entire world ever be run under the law of love? Why or why not?
3. What does it mean to believe in the kingdom of God?

Questions for Dialogue with Non-Christians

1. What does faith mean in your tradition?
2. Do you view the Christian belief in the law of love to be naive, attractive, or hypocritical? Why?
3. Where does love fit into your vision of the world as it should be?

The kingdom of God . . .

. . . is freedom from fear.

What are we humans afraid of? Death, certainly. Suffering, of course—of ourselves or our loved ones. We are afraid of a lot of other things as well, such as being wrong about something important, not being part of the in crowd, making a fool of ourselves, missing the opportunity of a lifetime, not making a difference with our lives, being forgotten—the list is long and familiar.

The good news of the kingdom of God is that we don't have to fear any of that. After his death and resurrection, Jesus appeared to his disciples several times and greeted them with "Do not be afraid" (Matthew 14:27; Mark 6:50; Luke 12:32; John 6:20) and "Peace be with you" (John 20:19, 21, 26).

When I was a child, this made perfect sense to me. If you see someone you know has died—especially if it was a gruesome, senseless death—then being afraid is a logical response, and the "ghost" you are encountering needs to reassure you that everything is all right. Apparently, that's what happened with the disciples.

As I grew older, however, I realized that ghosts were the least of my problems. I was afraid of a lot of things, most of them not supernatural at all. I began to see that Jesus was not admonishing his disciples not to be afraid of *him*. He was telling them that there was *nothing* left to be afraid of.

What does it mean not to be afraid of anything? In the world as it is, of course, this is pretty foolish. There are a lot of things to fear, and rightly so. For example, we're afraid that global warming might destroy our entire planet. That fear prompts the nations of the world to action they might not take otherwise.

We fear for our children's safety. That's why we teach them to look both ways before they cross a street, and never to drive after they drink alcohol. This can save them from tragedy, even though we know that accidents can still happen. And so parents are afraid.

We fear we will lose our jobs, so we work harder. We fear we will elect the wrong leaders, so we get involved in politics. We're afraid that if we cheat on our spouse it will lead to divorce, badly damaging our families, so we remain faithful.

But in the kingdom of God, in the world as it should be, we aren't supposed to be afraid. The difference is that we are at peace. It is peace that comes directly from following Jesus of Nazareth, the Anointed One. This peace is not the same as the absence of conflict; surely Christ's followers encounter conflict in a world that does not understand the kingdom. But followers of Jesus can experience a deep and abiding sense that, ultimately, everything will turn out all right.

This peace comes on two levels. One is spiritual and the other existential.

On the spiritual level, Christians believe that Jesus overcame death. When someone rises from the dead, there's really not much left to fear: that is why we Christians cling so strongly to a belief in life after death for everyone. When you believe that death is not the end of your existence, that you will continue to live on in a real, conscious way and will be reunited with your loved ones in heaven, then it is pretty difficult to be completely afraid of suffering and death. Of course, we're somewhat fearful of things on a human level; Jesus himself cried out on the cross, "My God, my God, why have you abandoned me?" (Matthew 27:46). But our belief in the kingdom of God includes no fear at the deepest level of our souls. Jesus conquered death; he promised we would do the same, and that is good enough for us.

It is not just our belief in an afterlife that gives Christians courage, however. The kingdom of God is a this-worldly vision, and as soon as we embrace that vision, our fear begins to leave. Christians firmly believe that the kingdom of God is God's plan for the world. Therefore we are convinced it *will happen*, sooner or later. We also know that God will bring it about, so we don't have to worry about making mistakes or failing in our efforts. This frees us up to try new and harder things, to take risks where they don't appear justified, and to love others when they don't (or can't) return love to us.

St. Francis of Assisi used to call himself a fool for Christ, and every Christian is in some way a fool. We believe in a world that has never existed, at least on earth, and we are willing to work to help bring about that world—despite the odds against it. We do so because we are not afraid. On an existential level—that is, on the level of our experience—we know that none of the things we fear is as important as our mission in life. At the end of every

Catholic Mass, the priest or deacon sends the entire congregation to "go in peace to love and serve the Lord," and the entire congregation answers, "Thanks be to God!"

Christians are charged with carrying out the work of Jesus; we are invited to be partners with God the Creator in helping to create the kingdom of God here on earth. With that as our purpose and God as our company, what can we possibly fear?

Questions for Christians

1. Other than the death or suffering of you or your loved ones, what are you most afraid of? Make a list.
2. What do you think Jesus meant when he told us not to be afraid? What, exactly, is the peace that he gives?
3. Think of a human purpose that has curbed your fear—such as the purpose to protect your family or to make a public claim to justice. What does such purpose do inside you that causes fear to recede? What is the relationship between your purpose as a Christian and your level of fear or anxiety?

Questions for Dialogue with Non-Christians

1. What is most to be feared in your tradition? What are some examples?
2. How does your tradition teach people to overcome fear? What does "peace be with you" mean in your tradition?
3. Do you observe most Christians as being more afraid or less afraid of things than most people? To what do you attribute this?

25

The kingdom of God . . .

. . . *is not sexist.*

J esus was a Jew of the first century. It is helpful to remember that when we are looking at his vision of the world as it should be.

Some Christians today want to emphasize the divine nature of Jesus and so assume that he could foresee and understand all the social and political and scientific developments over the centuries. For these people, Jesus' humanity was almost like a suit of clothes that he wore over his true identity as the Son of God or, simply, God.

This was actually a big fight in the early Christian church, because there was an equally strong group that wanted to emphasize that Jesus was a real human being, one who would have been the product of his times like all the rest of us. This Jesus would have learned things he did not know and "increased in wisdom and in years, and in divine and human favor" (Luke 2:52). He would have put his pants on one leg at a time and—here is the important point—looked at things the way his fellow Jews did. There are a lot of Christians around today who come down on the side of this understanding of Jesus.

The early church fathers split the difference. After about three hundred years of thinking and arguing about it, they came to an understanding (spelled out clearly in the Nicene Creed, which is accepted by almost all Christian denominations even today) that Jesus had two natures, one human and one divine, that existed in him at all times simultaneously. In the opening to the Gospel of John, it is stated this way:

> The Word was God,
> > in readiness for God from day one. . . .
> The Word became flesh and blood,
> > and moved into the neighborhood.
>
> JOHN 1:1, 14, *THE MESSAGE*

Why is it so important for us to make this distinction about Jesus being two natures at once? Because if we understand the distinction, we will have a different take on what Jesus said about his kingdom and how and why he said it the way he did.

The kingdom of God is the product of a person who was intimately in touch with God and God's plan for the world; he was also completely in touch with his own humanness. So, the kingdom of God is a divine idea proclaimed by a human person, one who was a first-century Jewish man, the product of his own time and culture.

On the surface, it looks as if Jesus' kingdom is for and by men. God is, after all, referred to as Father. It is a "king"-dom. The original inner circle is made up of twelve men (albeit one of them doesn't work out so well). The writers of all the sacred Christian texts that were allowed into the Bible (by men) are all presumed to be men. And the initial church institutions in both the eastern and western parts of the Roman Empire were, and continue to be, controlled by men. How can this not be called sexist?

Well, Jesus was a Jewish man of the first century. How else would you expect him to talk about God and his vision of how the world should be? Who else but men would you think he would have recruited as his key followers? What kind of a church might you have expected those followers to build? Of course Jesus would have called it a kingdom. (Did you expect him to call it a representational democracy or a queenship)? Of course he would refer to God as male. (Did you expect him to conceive of God as female?) Of course his key followers would have been male. (Did you expect him to pick women for key roles in that day and age?) The only thing surprising would have been if Jesus had done the opposite. Because then he would not have been a product of his times, and therefore he would not have been a real human being, because all humans are products of their times.

So, was Jesus sexist? Well, let's look at how he actually lived and taught his kingdom of God. As the author Susan Matthews points out, in many ways his was a feminine view of the world as it should be. He used a lot of feminine images for God and the kingdom—a hen gathering her chicks under her wings (see Matthew 23:37), for example, and those who receive a child (see Luke 9:48), which would have been primarily women, at least in those days. For Jesus, women exemplified the world as it should be in many extraordinary ways.

It is critical to note that women were key disciples and involved with Jesus' life from beginning to end. Start with his mother, Mary. What an extraordinary person. The story of the Annunciation practically gives her credit for the Incarnation. She clearly had a choice: give birth to the divine or say no and lead a normal life.

She chose to follow the will of God. "Yes, I see it all now," she says to the angel. "I am the Lord's maid, ready to serve. Let it be with me just as you say" (Luke 1:38, *The Message*).

It is Mary who gets her reluctant son (who, at the age of thirty, was already an older adult for the times) to finally begin his public ministry. What is interesting is her choice of venue and issue: the wedding of a friend of hers, to which Jesus and his friends had been invited also. The problem was a simple, human one. The wedding party had not bought enough wine. You wouldn't think this worthy of Jesus' first miracle, but Mary had her own vision of the kingdom of God, and it obviously included having a good time and helping out friends in a bind—no matter how mundane.

Mary doesn't play a big part in the Gospels, but she is around for several big moments. First of all, it is she and her husband, Joseph, who raise Jesus to be who he was meant to be. Anyone who has been a parent knows that the importance of this cannot be overestimated. Second, she is there at the Crucifixion—one of only four people mentioned at the foot of the cross, three women and one man. And she is specifically mentioned as being present at Pentecost, when the fledgling church received the Holy Spirit and finally got enough courage to go out and start proclaiming the kingdom of God.

There is another Mary who played a huge role in the early church, Mary of Magdala. She was named as one of the woman who supported the ministry of Jesus financially, she was present at the foot of the cross as well, and—most important—she was the first disciple to encounter the risen Christ and to try to convince the other disciples that it was true. History has not treated Mary of Magdala kindly. The Gospel attributed to her did not make it into the canon of the Bible. Her activities after the Resurrection were not documented the way that Peter's and Paul's and other men's were. One pope (Gregory the Great in 591) lumped her together with other women in the Gospels, including the woman caught in adultery and the woman who washed Jesus' feet with her tears. Popular culture has speculated that Mary of Magdala was a love interest of Jesus or even his wife and the mother of his children. But the bottom line is that she was a key follower of Jesus, one who is called "the apostle to the apostles." If the early church could have ignored her, they probably would have, but they couldn't because of how important she was.

There are multiple other women in the Gospels who played a key role in Jesus' life and mission: the sisters Mary and Martha; the unnamed Samaritan woman at the well; the Canaanite woman who confronted Jesus and convinced him that his kingdom was meant for all people, not just the Jews. What is amazing is not that there are so few women mentioned in the Scripture but that they are mentioned at all. They are mentioned because they were important influences on Jesus (as he was on them) who helped him develop and proclaim his vision for the world. Jesus, who knew God's intent for the world intimately, recognized the contributions of women to the building of the kingdom and went out of his way to encourage them. His example obviously heightened the awareness of the early church, including those who wrote the Scriptures. The fact that the church has often sinned in its treatment of women over the centuries is no fault of his.

We have to remember this: the kingdom of God is *not* the church. The church is meant to proclaim the kingdom, but the kingdom is in and for the world. And that kingdom is for everyone, without distinction. As Paul put it: "In Christ's family there can be no division into Jew and non-Jew, slave and free, male and female. Among us you are all equal" (Galatians 3:28, *The Message*).

Although the church may have been (and may continue to be) patriarchal and sexist, the kingdom of God has never been and never can be. Jesus was a product of his times, but his vision of the kingdom of God was for all time and all people.

Questions for Christians

1. If Jesus was the product of his times, how would that have affected his view of women and his images of God and his choice of key followers?
2. How did Jesus actually treat women? What does that teach us about the kingdom of God?
3. Do you think the kingdom of God could allow for any inequality or discrimination? Why or why not?

Questions for Dialogue with Non-Christians

1. What has been the view of women in your tradition? Have they always been considered equal to men? Why or why not? What women were important figures in the development of your tradition?
2. Do you observe that Christians are committed to the equality of men and women in the world? What are some examples?
3. In your vision of the world as it should be, what does equality mean?

The kingdom of God . . .

. . . *is not patronizing.*

Jesus' vision of the way the world should be is good news for the poor and oppressed. It is about freedom and equality and justice for all. That is clear and inarguable. This is why people who view themselves as political and social liberals are so drawn to it.

But those who are of a more conservative bent socially and politically also have cause for cheer, because it is also obvious that the kingdom of God is not some welfare state in which we are all given whatever we need or want. The kingdom of God is not a free lunch. We have to work for it.

The key to understanding this apparent contradiction is that, in Jesus' mind, the kingdom of God, the world as it should be, is not built on the goodwill of those in power. It is built on the will of God, who is never patronizing.

What does God want for us? Jesus is very sure: "The Father wants to give you the very kingdom itself" (Luke 12:32, *The Message*).

But the kingdom does not come without effort on our part. Near the end of the Sermon on the Mount, Jesus says: "Don't look for shortcuts to God. The market is flooded with surefire, easygoing formulas for a successful life that can be practiced in your spare time. Don't fall for that stuff, even though crowds of people do. The way to life—to God!—is vigorous and requires total attention" (Matthew 7:13–14, *The Message*).

The kingdom of God is one of grace freely given and available to all, surely, but it is also one of personal responsibility and action: "Not everyone who says to me, 'Lord, Lord,' will enter the kingdom of heaven, but only the one who does the will of my Father in heaven" (Matthew 7:21). Jesus said that the kingdom is like a person who builds a home on solid rock instead of sand. When the rain comes, the house will stand instead of being washed away. It is like a woman who has ten coins and loses one of them. She spends the entire day sweeping the house until she finds it. It is like a priceless pearl, for which you sell everything to buy.

What does all this mean for us? Well, it means that we aren't supposed to be sitting around waiting for God (or anybody else) to make the world a better place. That is clearly our job. God wants the kingdom to happen, and we have been assured of all the support we need to help bring it about. But we must work at it, not expect it to be handed to us.

Also, "thy kingdom come" means that good intentions are not enough. We are not supposed to merely *try* to make the world more like the way God would have it. We are supposed to succeed. That is kind of a scary thought, given the state of the world and how far we are from the way it should be. But Jesus repeatedly made it clear that he was serious. "If you don't go all the way with me, through thick and thin, you don't deserve me. If your first concern is to look after yourself, you'll never find yourself. But if you forget about yourself and look to me, you'll find both yourself and me" (Matthew 10:38–39, *The Message*).

And the kingdom means that we cannot patronize or be patronized; we cannot do for others what they can do for themselves or allow others to do things for us that we should be doing for ourselves: "In everything do to others as you would have them do to you; for this is the law and the prophets" (Matthew 7:12). This is a cardinal rule of community organizing, the kind Barack Obama did before he was elected president. It says that all people—especially the poor and the oppressed—need to take their lives into their own hands. This is radical stuff, but it is neither liberal nor conservative. It says that the poor and the oppressed must participate in their own liberation, that they cannot afford to allow themselves to become dependent on others—the government, the church, or do-gooders. For if the poor and the oppressed do not participate in the building of the world as it should be, then that world will never be the kingdom of God.

What is it about the kingdom of God that is so controversial? You'd think that everyone would want to live by the law of love as soon as they realized it was possible. What is controversial is that *love is work*. It does not just happen because we want it to. It comes with a price, and that price is steep. Love costs ego and power and prestige and money and position. It means that the first become last and the last become first. It means taking off your suit coat and washing the feet of friend and betrayer alike. It means respecting others, including their view of the world as it should be.

Here is how Matthew described people's reaction to the Sermon on the Mount, where Jesus laid out this nonpatronizing prescription for how we are to live: "When Jesus concluded his address, the crowd burst into applause. They had never heard teaching like this. It was apparent that he was living everything he was saying—quite a contrast to their religion teachers! This was the best teaching they had ever heard" (Matthew 7:28–29, *The Message*).

Questions for Christians

1. If you could simply hand people the kingdom of God, would you do it? Why or why not?
2. What is the difference between something you work for and something that is done for you? Which do you value more, and why?
3. What is the cost of love? What are some examples?

Questions for Dialogue with Non-Christians

1. What demands does your tradition put on people? Why?
2. How do you view the difference between helping people and empowering them? Which is better? Why?
3. If the world could live the law of love, would that be enough for you? Why or why not?

The kingdom of God . . .

. . . *is expensive.*

If Jesus was clear about one thing, it was that the kingdom of God would not be accepted easily and that both he and his followers would suffer because of it: "I've come to start a fire on this earth—how I wish it were blazing right now! I've come to change everything, turn everything rightside up—how I long for it to be finished! Do you think I came to smooth things over and make everything nice? Not so. I've come to disrupt and confront!" (Luke 12:49–51, *The Message*).

On the surface, it's not clear why this would be so. First of all, Jesus' vision of the world as it should be was one of brotherly love and inner peace. Christianity was not to be coercive—people were not to be forced to enter the kingdom of God, nor were the followers of Jesus supposed to impose their ideas on others. To tell the truth, Jesus didn't seem to have much of a concrete plan for bringing about the kingdom of God.

Second, the newly named "Christians" went around doing good: healing the sick, taking care of widows and orphans, and helping the poor. Who wouldn't want a group like that around, cleaning up the debris left by society?

Third, the early Christians weren't a particularly political people. They certainly weren't revolutionaries in the sense that Samuel Adams or Leon Trotsky or Mother Jones were revolutionaries. The Christians had no weapons, armies, or ideology—other than that of the kingdom of God, which by Jesus' own admission would not be like other kingdoms in the world, with armies to protect it.

So, what was it about God's way of doing things that was so threatening to the status quo that those in power had to kill Jesus and then persecute his followers? And what, if anything, makes the kingdom of God an idea so dangerous that even present-day followers of Jesus might be persecuted for speaking about it freely and enthusiastically?

It's important to remember that I am not referring to various efforts of Christians over the centuries to develop secular power and impose their beliefs on others. This started with the Roman emperor Constantine, continued through the Middle Ages, and still exists today. Such forced imposition of the kingdom of God is a perversion and rightly deserves to be suspected, opposed, and defeated by those who do not share the Christian view of the world as it should be.

But that was not the situation when Jesus was put to death. The world as God would have it is peaceful, loving, open, noncoercive, nonjudgmental, and collaborative—all characteristics that Jesus lived out and demonstrated consistently. Why is this kind of approach to the world as it should be still threatening to others? Why do Christians today—people who have given up all intention of forcing others to believe what they believe—still attract opposition?

Perhaps it is because the kingdom of God turns everything on its head. It puts the last first and the first last. It favors those who are most despised and oppressed. It returns good for evil. When you do these things, you challenge the conventional wisdom, the status quo. And when you do that, people get angry and fight back.

This is why some Christians, those working hard to live out God's kingdom, are still persecuted. In some situations, that persecution is brutal and deadly—we remember, for example, Archbishop Óscar Romero and the Maryknoll and Jesuit martyrs killed in El Salvador, or Sister Dorothy Stange, the fighter for the rights of the indigenous people in Brazil. But for most Christians, the cost of the kingdom is not so much physical danger as it is economic, social, and religious isolation or discrimination.

What is the economic cost of living God's kingdom? You can't fully embrace either capitalist or socialist ideology. That is, you can't trust the free market system or the government to do the right thing at all times, and so you have to step outside both of them at times to accomplish God's will for the world. This tends to upset the people who are in power economically. And they will fight back.

Also, if you believe the kingdom of God to be the blueprint for the world as it should be, then you might not be able to be as wealthy as you'd like. Jesus said, "Do you have any idea how difficult it is for the rich to enter God's kingdom? Let me tell you, it's easier to gallop a camel through a needle's eye than for the rich to enter God's kingdom" (Matthew 19: 23–24, *The Message*). It may well be that the demands of the kingdom require you to share more of your money with poor people, or to pay your employees a higher wage, or to refrain from cheating on your taxes (or maybe not pay them at all if they are unjust). All of this can cost you economically.

Socially, the kingdom has costs as well. Perhaps it will move you to adopt a handicapped child (or bring one to term), or oppose a particular social policy, or befriend prisoners or people with AIDS or some other group at the bottom of the social scale. This can not only make you suspect by those in your own social group but also cause problems with immediate family members, relatives, and friends. They may not exactly persecute you, but they certainly might ostracize you.

Socially, too, you might suffer for your political positions. Perhaps you will be viewed as too conservative, or too liberal, or too radical. You may be stereotyped as permissive or restrictive. Your kids or your spouse might not agree with everything you do. Jesus even said that the kingdom would pit brother against brother, parent against child (see Matthew 10:12; Mark 13:12).

In terms of religious life, there is also a price to pay. This may seem odd, especially if we are talking about a Christian church or denomination, but just as Jesus angered the religious leaders of his day, you may find your religious leaders not as tolerant of your views or actions as you would hope. By its very nature, organized religion worries about rules and doctrines, and the kingdom of God puts rules and doctrines second to the law of love.

So, if you think, for example, that in the world as it should be men and women should be equal in all things, this might put you in conflict with religious leaders who say that women are not allowed to be ordained in the church. If you stand up for what you believe, you may be persecuted (for example, excommunicated) by the very church leaders who are supposed to help you bring about the kingdom of God. You still have to do it, of course, because that is the nature of the kingdom.

Is all this cost worth it? Jesus certainly thought it was. He said the kingdom of God was like a pearl of great price (see Matthew 13:46). Generations of Christians have felt that the pearl was more than worth the sacrifice it takes to purchase it. It is up to you to decide for yourself, however. The one thing you can be pretty sure of, though, is that if the kingdom isn't costing you anything, you really aren't trying very hard to bring it about.

Questions for Christians

1. What are three things—one economic, one social, and one in your religious community—that your belief in the kingdom of God costs you? If you can't think of anything, what does that say to you?
2. If the kingdom of God really costs you, is it worth it? Why or why not?
3. If we Christians aren't trying to force other people to make the world the way we think it should be, why do they still oppose our efforts?

Questions for Dialogue with Non-Christians

1. Do your beliefs cost you in any way? How?
2. Do you fear that Christians are trying to impose their views on you? Why, and how do you react?
3. Could you work with Christians to make the world as it should be while disagreeing on certain goals and methods? Explain.

The kingdom of God . . .

. . . *pays off big.*

I f the kingdom of God potentially costs so much, why be part of it? Well, it does cost a lot, but it also pays off big in many ways.

Jesus was not shy about talking about this payoff, although over the centuries his promise of eternal life seems to be the one most remembered. But the kingdom of God is primarily a plan for this world, and as such, it has immediate payoffs here and now.

The first payoff is for Christians themselves. Jesus promised us what every human being is looking for: happiness, acceptance, and community. Christians are supposed to love one another, and if they don't, then something is wrong with their understanding of or approach to the world as it should be. One of the early church leaders, Tertullian, wrote that non-Christians described the early Christians this way: "'Look how they love one another' (for [the pagans] themselves hate one another); 'and how they are ready to die for one another' (for the pagans themselves are readier to kill one another).'" Who wouldn't be attracted to a group like the early Christians? Obviously, many were and still are.

Followers of Jesus who believe in the kingdom of God also receive another thing that all humans crave: a sense of purpose, a mission worthy of their lives. This is no small thing in a world that many believe operates on the basis of the idea that whoever has the most things when he or she dies wins. Who would want to live life with such a silly goal?

Christians also have a sense of relief that the world does not have to be and will not always be the way it is. When we see suffering and injustice, it certainly affects us. We may be sad and outraged, but we are not complacent or depressed. We have a plan, and we are part of the plan. The good news that Christians preach is not only that God is going to bring about the world as it should be but also that we ourselves are part of that effort. Christians fully believe that we are part of the solution, even as we confess that we are also part of the problem.

Jesus had many stories that demonstrated the big payoff the kingdom of God brings. In his first parable in the Gospel of Mark, he tells the story of a farmer who planted seeds (see Mark 4:1–9). Some of the seeds fell on the road and birds ate them. Some fell in poor soil and didn't put down roots, so they withered and died. Some fell among weeds and were strangled by them. But some fell on good ground and produced a harvest that was thirty or sixty or a hundred times as much as was scattered. Later, Jesus explained this parable to his disciples: "You've been given insight into God's kingdom—you know how it works. . . . The seed planted in the good earth represents those who hear the Word, embrace it, and produce a harvest beyond their wildest dreams" (Mark 4:11, 20, *The Message*).

So, whatever we Christians give up for the kingdom, we know that the payoff is great. "What good would it do to get everything you want and lose you, the real you?" Jesus asked. "This isn't, you realize, pie in the sky by and by. Some who have taken their stand right here are going to see it happen, see with their own eyes the kingdom of God" (Luke 9:25, 27, *The Message*).

There is one other entity that gets a big payoff from the kingdom of God, and that's the world itself. The world needs a plan if it is not going to self-destruct. It appears that we humans are perfectly capable of destroying the entire planet, and if we do that, we may well also destroy what we call intelligent life in the universe. This very real threat comes not only from global warming or a population explosion or nuclear war or infectious disease but also from poverty and ethnic hatred and religious intolerance.

This world needs not only to survive but also to thrive in the foreseeable future. It may be that humans someday leave our home planet and populate the stars. Then we will need a plan for the *universe as it should be*. Fortunately, we have a plan, one that we Christians consider God's own plan, revealed to us by God's own Son.

Having such a plan is a huge gift. We now know how we human beings are supposed to relate to one another and to our environment. We have been shown how we are supposed to help bring this new world about, and we have been given the tools to do so. It is not necessary that everyone agree with this particular Christian view. It is only important that we Christians do, for the concept and reality of the kingdom of God is our main contribution to the human enterprise.

The way Jesus put it is that we Christians are to be salt of the earth and a light to the nations:

> Does anyone bring a lamp home and put it under a washtub or beneath the bed? Don't you put it up on a table or on the mantle? We're not keeping secrets, we're telling them; we're not hiding things, we're bringing them out into the open. . . .

Listen carefully to what I am saying—and be wary of the shrewd advice that tells you how to get ahead in the world on your own. Giving, not getting, is the way. Generosity begets generosity. Stinginess impoverishes.

MARK 4:21–22, 24–25, *THE MESSAGE*

The kingdom of God is a plan for the world as it should be and comes equipped with a group of people committed to help bring it about. This is indeed good news and a big payoff.

Questions for Christians

1. What is the biggest payoff you personally receive from your participation in the kingdom of God? How does it compare with what you put into it?
2. If the kingdom of God comes, why will that be good for the world?
3. In what ways are you salt of the earth and a light to the nations? What are some examples?

Questions for Dialogue with Non-Christians

1. What is your vision for the world as it should be? Where does it come from? Who shares this vision with you? How does it differ from the Christian view of the kingdom of God?
2. What is your personal payoff for being involved in helping to bring about a better world?
3. If your vision of the world as it should be becomes reality, why is that a good thing for everyone?

The kingdom of God . . .

. . . is eternal.

Much of the difficulty we have in understanding Jesus' concept of the kingdom of God lies in the misconception that it is about what happens after our death. The phrase that is used in Christian circles most often to imply this next-worldly view is "eternal life." But *Webster's Unabridged International Dictionary* defines *eternal* as "without beginning or end." *Eternal* is not the same as *immortal*. What Jesus offers us is not mere immortality (although it may well include that) but life that has no beginning *and* no end.

For example, during Jesus' famous conversation with the Samaritan woman at Jacob's well, he promises her that he can give her "living water."

> The woman said, "Sir, you don't even have a bucket to draw with, and this well is deep. So how are you going to get this 'living water'? Are you a better man than our ancestor Jacob, who dug this well and drank from it, he and his sons and livestock, and passed it down to us?"

> Jesus said: "Everyone who drinks this water will get thirsty again and again. Anyone who drinks the water I give will never thirst—not ever. The water I give will be an artesian spring within, gushing fountains of endless life."
>
> JOHN 4:11–14, *THE MESSAGE*

In other words, the kingdom of God is something that is always there, always available. It always has been, and always will be. We just have to tap into it.

In our efforts to help bring about the world as it should be, what are the practical effects of believing that the kingdom of God is eternal? If we really believe it is eternal, then that means we don't have to wait to experience God's kingdom. It is here for the asking, right now. Nor do we need permission from anyone to drink from the well or wait until we die before the kingdom of God can come into being. We also don't have to worry about failing to bring the kingdom about. It has no beginning; it has no end; it is, has been, and always will be present.

To say that the kingdom of God is eternal means that it is beyond the realm of humanity. It is divine, that is, "of God." This eternal nature of the kingdom of God is what gives Christians such confidence (in the face of so much evidence to the contrary) that the kingdom of God will ultimately win out. In one sense, we can't mess it up. Because it has no beginning and no end, it must succeed eventually. Our job, like that of the woman at the well, is merely to drink from the water Jesus offers (i.e., the kingdom of God) and we will receive endless life. What happens then, of course, is that—just like the woman at the well—we become missionaries for this new vision of the way the world should be (see John 4:39–42).

All this may seem esoteric and theoretical, so let me give an example. I run a small business. We publish and distribute books on religion, baseball, and community organizing (because those are the things I am interested in). We have a dozen employees and semipermanent freelancers, plus a lot of authors. The question is, can a company be run the way God would have it run, the way a company should be run in the kingdom of God?

The answer is yes and no. This depends on whether the kingdom of God is eternal, and it depends on what we mean by *should*.

No, we cannot run a company the way God would have things—we'd probably go out of business. Yet there is no doubt that, if we want to, we can run a company that possesses many aspects or flashes of the kingdom of God.

If the kingdom of God has no beginning or end, then the possibility of running our business on its principles always exists. We can tap into it anytime we want. In fact, if we keep at it we will eventually succeed, because in an eternal world, there is always time to accomplish something.

If what we mean by *should* is that we are expected to be perfect at all times in everything we do, then obviously we cannot run a business that way. If *should* means that our goal, our intention, our effort in running our company is to run it as a little pocket of the kingdom of God, then of course we can do it—and we should.

Take any other situation and ask the question of whether it can be dealt with in a kingdom-of-God or a world-as-it-should-be way, and you will see that the answer is always the same as in my workplace example.

For instance, can we raise our children to be conscientious citizens of the kingdom of God? Yes and no. Yes, if we are willing to take little victories. No, if they have to be perfect. If we have an eternity, though, we should succeed, but that depends on what we mean by *should*.

Go ahead. Try it for yourself. Think of any situation or activity that you are involved in, and ask yourself if it could become an expression of the kingdom of God.

Questions for Christians

1. In what ways can you bring about the kingdom of God in your home, community, and workplace? What if you had unlimited time and opportunities?
2. What is the living water Jesus offered to the woman at the well? Have you ever drunk it? Explain.
3. What are the differences between eternity and immortality?

Questions for Dialogue with Non-Christians

1. How does your tradition view time? How does that view influence your efforts to make the world a better place?
2. What do you think Jesus might have meant when he offered "living water" to the woman at the well?
3. What does *should* mean in your tradition? What are some examples?

The kingdom of God . . .

. . . *is true.*

I s the kingdom of God true? The answer to this question is ultimately the answer to the question that Pontius Pilate asked Jesus during their famous exchange.

Pilate asked Jesus if he was a king.

Jesus answered that his kingdom is not of this world, because if it were organized according to the world's values, his followers would have fought to protect him, and they did not.

So Pilate asked Jesus again if he was a king, and he said he was: "Because I am King, I was born and entered the world so that I could witness to the truth. Everyone who cares for truth, who has any feeling for the truth, recognizes my voice" (John 18:37, *The Message*).

So, there it is. Jesus' view of the kingdom of God—the way the world should be—is true to the extent that he correctly understood and lived the way God wants humans to live. "I am the Road, also the Truth, also the Life," he says earlier in the Gospel of John. "If you really knew me, you would know my Father as well. . . . The words that I speak to you aren't mere words. I don't just make them up on my own" (John 14:6, 9, 10, *The Message*).

What, exactly, was Jesus' vision for the world? To simplify, it is the law of love. "Let me give you a new command," Jesus told them. "Love one another. In the same way I loved you, you love one another. This is how everyone will recognize that you are my disciples—when they see the love you have for each other" (John 13:34–35, *The Message*).

And why do we Christians think his view is the true one? We think so for two reasons. One is the testimony of his disciples. The other is our own experience.

The original disciples were an unlikely and difficult-to-trust group. They seemed especially dense in understanding what Jesus was trying to propose. They were constantly making assumptions and going off in wrong directions, only to be brought back by Jesus. Apparently, the kingdom of God was such a radical concept that they couldn't fathom it. (This is comforting for us contemporary disciples who also have a difficult time fathoming that the world could be the way Jesus described it. We have proved equally dense.)

It was the resurrection of Jesus from the dead and the disciples' encounters with him after he had been raised that finally made them believers—so much so that they became a courageous band of missionaries that took Jesus' message to the ends of the earth. What they wanted people to know was that Jesus was totally innocent of any charges against him, except that he clung to his belief in the nature of God and God's plan for the world. For this he was put to death in a most gruesome way. But he went to his death without compromising what he knew to be true: that God loves us and that we are to love one another.

Had Jesus never risen from the dead, then none of us would have heard of him and his improbable idea. But he did, at least in the experience of his followers, beginning with Mary of Magdala and including Peter, Thomas, and a latecomer named Saul (who was later called Paul). One of them was John, who ended his Gospel this way: "This is the disciple who is testifying to these things and has written them, and we know that his testimony is true" (John 21:24).

What the disciples testified to was that this one man, who seemed to have personal knowledge of the way God would have things, actually lived what he taught, right up until the end when he was killed for his beliefs. Yet he never stopped believing, because he knew that what he was saying was the truth. And for that faithfulness, God raised up Jesus from the dead in a real way, one that they all experienced and then shared with the rest of us. That is one reason we believe that Jesus' idea of the kingdom of God is the way the world should be.

But there is another reason some of us believe. We believe it because we have experienced it ourselves. We have all experienced times when the world was in sync with the law of love. Maybe it doesn't happen often or last long, but there are times when we say, "If the entire world could operate this way, what a great world it would be." It may have been in an encounter with a parent or spouse or child or sibling or friend or stranger; it may have been at work, when someone treated us justly or we did the same for someone else; it may have been at church, when we put the needs of others before our own; it may have been in our community or civic or political affairs, when we stood for the whole and worked for the common good instead of for our selfish interests. Whenever and wherever it happened, we experienced the kingdom of God, and we *knew* it to be true.

Let us say one last time that we are not going to impose this view of the world as it should be on anyone else. Jesus offered it to Pilate, and Pilate was tempted by it, but in the end, Pilate rejected it in favor of political expediency. Jesus didn't try to force it on him. He merely accepted the consequences of Pilate's rejection of his dream for the world, but he never gave up his belief that his vision was the right one.

Pilate asked him, "What is truth?" (John 18:38).

Jesus replied with his life. His vision for the world is true. It is the way the world should be.

Questions for Christians

1. How would you define truth?
2. What is God's true vision for how the world should be? How do you know?
3. When and how have you experienced the kingdom of God being present in your life? What are some specific examples, with dates, times, and places? Who else was there?

Questions for Dialogue with Non-Christians

1. Please answer Pilate's question: "What is truth?" How is it determined in your tradition?
2. What do you know for sure about how the world should be? Where do you get that knowledge? Why do you believe it is true?
3. Does it offend you that Christians believe that their vision of the world as it should be is true? Why or why not? How can you work with Christians to incorporate your view with theirs? How can Christians work with you to incorporate their view with yours?

Conclusion

Where do we go from here? If we Christians believe that the kingdom of God is a real plan for how the world should be, then we have to take it seriously—on our jobs; with our families and loved ones; and in our civic, community, and political involvement.

We also have to figure out, in practical terms, how we help bring about the kingdom. We will always live between the world as it is and the world as it should be. How do we operate in the world of imperfection and compromise without losing sight of our ideals, and how do we live in heaven on earth without getting totally out of touch with reality?

The answer is that we need the church, a community of fellow believers that is constantly reminding us that the kingdom has already begun but is not yet fully realized. We need to support and challenge one another to keep our faith and hope in the vision of Jesus for this world.

We also need to have dialogues with our fellow Christians of all denominations about what Jesus really had in mind for this here-and-now kingdom, which is to come on earth just as it is in heaven.

That is why I have offered questions at the end of each chapter for reflection and discussion among Christians. I'd love to see small groups grapple with these questions in a real way. For my part, I will continue to speak and write about this issue. I maintain the Internet discussion group Faith and Work in Cyberspace. If you'd like to join, send me an e-mail at SpiritualityWork@aol.com.

Finally, we need to get into dialogue with those of other faiths and secular traditions about the world as it should be. They will have their own ideas and images for talking about this, and we owe it to them to share ours and listen to theirs. Who knows where this will lead? That is why I included questions at the end of each chapter for dialogue with non-Christians. I would be pleased and honored if small groups of people of all faiths who are interested in a better world used this book as a starting place for understanding one another and coming up with new ways to work together for the common good.

So, I'll meet you in the kingdom—not just after we die (although that would be nice, too) but right now. The world the way God would have it has already begun, but it has never been completely and permanently accomplished. It is our job to make that happen.

Acknowledgments

I have to confess that this is the strangest book I have ever written, in the sense that it almost wrote itself. I began with a simple premise: the kingdom of God is the Christian way of talking about the world as it should be. From there, it was just a matter of saying to myself, "What does that really mean in concrete terms?" It was amazing how easily the ideas came. I guess you could say I was inspired. But it was also a case of writing about what I have been taught and have practiced all my life.

So, I thank all the people who have influenced me over my sixty-some years, starting with my parents, Fran and Mary Pierce, and my seven siblings. (My eighty-five-year-old mom even proofread the manuscript for me.)

I also thank all the people who have taught me what I know and believe about the kingdom and the world as it should be, including my colleagues, teachers, and mentors at Maryknoll College, the Industrial Areas Foundation (especially Ed Chambers), the National Center for the Laity (especially Russ Barta, Ed Marciniak, and Bill Droel), the Coalition for Ministry in Daily Life (especially Pete Hammond), and United Power for Action and Justice. I also learned a lot from some of the great priests in the Archdiocese of Chicago, especially Bill Burke, Jack Egan, Don Headley, Bill Kenneally, and Leo Mahon, and from many great women in the church, both religious and lay, including Alice Camille, Kathleen Glavich, Amy Florian, Sue Matthews, and Mary Southard.

The people at Loyola Press have always been great to me. I want to mention them all, but I won't in fear of leaving someone out. They know who they are. But for this particular book I have to thank Joe Durepos, who made it happen, Vinita Wright, who is a superb editor and a much better writer than I am, and Katherine Faydash, who saved me from myself several times with her copyediting.

And thanks to John Shea for writing the foreword. He is my personal theologian, and any good ideas in this book are probably ultimately attributable to him.

My colleagues at ACTA Publications allow me a place to practice the spirituality of work every day, and they produce a lot of great material for the kingdom.

Finally, my wife, Kathy, and my three adult children, Abby, Nate, and Zack, are my rock. They give me great joy and hope for the future of this world. Kathy and I discussed every single idea in this book, and she has helped me understand the woman's view of the kingdom of God. It is my greatest hope that my kids will take up the cause of building the kingdom of God as their mission in life.

And to you, dear reader, I give thanks. I can't wait to see all the wonderful things you will do to make the world a better place. Jesus promised we would perform even greater miracles than he did. So, let's get to it!